Problem Solving, Reasoning and Numeracy in the Early Years Foundation Stage

Anita M. Hughes

Routledge
Taylor & Francis Group

LONDON AND NEW YORK

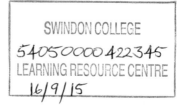

First published 2009
by Routledge
2 Park Square, Milton Park, Abingdon, Oxon OX14 4RN

Simultaneously published in the USA and Canada
by Routledge
711 Third Avenue, New York, NY 10017

Routledge is an imprint of the Taylor & Francis Group, an informa business

© 2009 Anita M. Hughes

Typeset in Optima by
Taylor & Francis Books

British Library Cataloguing in Publication Data
A catalogue record for this book is available from the British Library

Library of Congress Cataloging in Publication Data
Hughes, Anita M.
  Problem solving, reasoning and numeracy in the early years foundation
  stage / Anita M. Hughes.
    p. cm. – (Practical guidance in the EYFS)
  Includes bibliographical references.
  1. Problem solving–Study and teaching (Early childhood)–Activity programs.
  2. Reasoning–Study and teaching (Early childhood)–Activity programs.
  3. Numeracy–Study and teaching (Early childhood)–Activity programs.
  4. Early childhood education–Activity programs. 5. Problem solving in
  children. 6. Reasoning in children. I. Title.
  LB1139.35.A37H84 2008
370.15′24–dc22   2008026696

ISBN 978-0-415-47654-6 (pbk)
ISBN 978-0-415-47840-3 (hbk)

Problem Solving, Reasoning and Numeracy in the Early Years Foundation Stage

This book offers an in-depth understanding of children's thinking skills from a psychological perspective. The book introduces the learning tools model, a vital cognitive tool used by children to learn and solve problems, and gives practical ideas on how practitioners can use everyday materials to promote problem solving and early numeracy skills through play.

Readers are encouraged to reflect on their own practice and understanding to help them provide learning opportunities to meet the unique needs of all children in their setting.

Anita M. Hughes is a chartered educational psychologist.

Practical Guidance in the EYFS
Series Editor: Sandy Green

The *Practical Guidance in the EYFS* series will assist practitioners in the smooth and successful implementation of the Early Years Foundation Stage.

Each book gives clear and detailed explanations of each aspect of learning and development and encourages readers to consider each area within its broadest context to expand and develop their own knowledge and good practice.

Practical ideas and activities for all age groups are offered along with a wealth of expertise of how elements from the practice guidance can be implemented within all early years' settings. The books include suggestions for the innovative use of everyday resources, popular books and stories.

Titles in this series include:

To Holly and Emma

Contents

Acknowledgements

A book is never written without help and support, and this book is imbued with the love and enthusiasm of many people to whom I am truly grateful.

In particular, I would like to thank my husband Graham, who patiently read my drafts and uncomplainingly allowed me to 'disappear' every weekend and bank holiday for several months to work on this project.

My thanks are given to my friend and colleague Veronica Read, who supported me in my research as well as Jeanette Walker, Dilla Davies and Jo Ramatalla who shared ideas with me, which helped me to focus my thinking and to complete the work within the time schedule.

I also want to express special gratitude to June Smith of the Haven Children's Centre in Gosport and Pauline Brazier from the Alverbridge Pre-school, who allowed me to observe the children in their settings and provided me with some delightful photos. Their settings are wonderful examples of good practice.

I have also appreciated the stories of children shared by Paul and Karey Banwell, Barbara Robinson and Alix Griffiths, which gave me inspiration and joy throughout the writing process. Indeed, my gratitude is expressed for all the children who have delighted me with their play, curiosity, enthusiasm and daring over the years.

The theoretical ideas about the learning tools come from Katrin Stroh and Thelma Robinson, whose work I have admired since the early 1980s when I had the good fortune to be able to film some of the children they were working with. I would like to thank them for their friendship, encouragement, innovation and enthusiasm, which fuelled my enjoyment in researching for this book.

However, this book would never have been written without the inspiring work of Elinor Goldschmied, who conceived the idea of the 'treasure basket' and gave the name of 'heuristic play' to the exploratory play of toddlers. Her keen and questioning mind led to many animated discussions over twenty years and fostered an interest in the early years that has become a passion in my professional life.

Finally, I would like to thank my editor, Sandy Green, who was a constantly reassuring presence, sending me encouraging emails and guiding me throughout the project.

I hope that this book will help those working with the youngest children in our society to feel a renewed sense of confidence and pride in their work together with a desire to take the risk in trying out new ideas.

Introduction

Over the past twenty-five years I have found that whenever a group of early years practitioners are brought together, about half of them will tell you that they are 'bad at maths'. When asked how they know that they are bad at maths, the following reasons are given:

- My teacher said I was no good.
- I kept getting my sums wrong.
- I was in the lowest set.
- I came at the bottom in tests.

The perception of having poor number skills usually starts at school when children are propelled into using abstract symbols before they have securely understood the underlying mathematical concepts. Once we believe we have a difficulty with learning or doing something such as mathematical operations, it becomes a self-fulfilling prophecy as anxiety tarnishes the whole of our experience.

So what is this anxiety about? The anxiety is about two things:

1   the fear of failure;
2   the fear of disapproval or rejection from an authority figure.

The first 'sums' that are given to children at school often involve counting numbers and are imbued with rightness and wrongness. If they are asked to count out five objects, then there must be only five of them, not four or six. Rightness and wrongness conjures up judgement, and judgement produces feelings of fear. Children naturally seek approval and recognition from their parents, caregivers and teachers as a way of feeling secure. Indeed, secure relationships underpin all successful learning as Sue Gerhardt so vividly describes in her well-researched book *Why Love Matters* (2004).

Just as children need a secure base (in the form of loving relationships with key caregivers) in order to feel brave enough to explore and experiment in their play, so practitioners need the secure base of unambiguous support and guidance to be creative and experimental in their work. A guide is not an instructor but someone who points things out to you or points you on your way so you can learn and explore things for yourself.

For those working with very young children, anxieties are never far away as practitioners worry about whether or not they are 'doing the right thing' with the children in their settings. The Early Years Foundation Stage (EYFS) is a central part of the childcare strategy 'Choice for Parents, the Best Start for Children' and the Childcare Act (2006) and provides a coherent and flexible approach to care and learning for children from birth to five years. It is worth seeing the EYFS as a friendly guide to return to time and time again for support, reassurance and inspiration. We all need reassurance to feel confident and brave enough to take safe risks in being creative in our professional lives. This is because uncertainty and anxiety only lead to over-control or to taking no responsibility at all.

An illustration of this was described at a recent 'group problem-solving' exercise as part of a training workshop at which I was the facilitator. A practitioner, who was a room leader (of four people), expressed her sadness and frustration about her inability to engage her colleagues. She wanted to encourage a team approach and to get everyone involved. One member was new and understandably being cautious as she worked out the 'group norms' to fit in. Another member was an experienced practitioner who had only recently returned to childcare work after a long gap. The last member seemed disengaged and bored and spent much of the day using her mobile phone. How can this be, you may ask? Through the process of group problem-solving, where understanding rather than judgement was explored, it became apparent that the manager of this nursery was unconfident in her role of giving guidance. Instead, she was either unpredictably over-friendly, letting things 'go', such as turning a blind eye to the use of the phone, or over-authoritative in laying down strict and inflexible rules about the structure of the day. No wonder the staff were disengaged. They felt insecure, and the manager seemed unclear about and insecure in her role. This case study may sound extreme, but it is all too common in many settings reflecting the uncertainty about the underlying principles of care and learning for young children. The intention of the EYFS is not so much a curriculum directing you to work in a certain way, rather a 'containing' framework to support and guide you on your professional journey.

The delivery of the EYFS is mandatory from September 2008 in all schools and early years providers in Ofsted-registered settings attended by young children from birth to the end of the academic year in which they turn five. The EYFS acknowledges that multi-agency cooperation in partnership with parents underpins the process. The aim of the EYFS framework is to help children achieve the five Every Child Matters outcomes:

1   Be healthy.
2   Stay safe.
3   Enjoy and achieve.
4   Make a positive contribution.
5   Achieve economic well-being.

Alongside the *Statutory Framework for the Early Years Foundation Stage,* the Department for Education and Skills (DfES 2007a) has provided the *Practice Guidance for the Early Years Foundation Stage* (DfES 2007b), a document providing both information and advice within each of the six areas covered by early learning goals and educational programmes. The six areas are:

1   personal, social and emotional development;
2   communication, language and literacy;
3   problem-solving, reasoning and numeracy;
4   knowledge and understanding of the world;
5   physical development;
6   creative development.

The aim of this book is to support practitioners and students in the area that focuses on problem-solving, reasoning and numeracy. The content of this book will include:

●   an in-depth understanding of how children think and develop abstract concepts, which underpin all problem-solving and early numeracy skills;

- a historical perspective on how psychological research has changed our understanding of how children learn and has influenced government legislation on education and childcare;
- a clear presentation of heuristic play and the learning tools, which are vital cognitive tools, used by all children whatever their culture to learn and solve problems;
- additional ideas and resources for the practical implementation of this new legislation primarily through the use of everyday materials and experiences.

For the chapters which include practical ideas, this book has used the main headings from the practice guidance and has kept as closely as possible to its format. The main headings are:

- numbers as labels and for counting;
- calculating;
- shape, space and measures.

Each of these chapters (Chapters 6, 7 and 8) will relate to the full age range and will incorporate the early learning goals. The focus will be on encouraging and supporting practitioners to provide a wide range of ordinary, everyday and natural objects for children to explore and experience. Many young children spend most of their waking lives in childcare settings or urban environments, which are in danger of becoming alarmingly plastic and artificial as well as overly structured and monitored, so it is really important to offer 'home-like' experiences and everyday materials (household, natural and recycled) to enrich their lives.

It is hoped that practitioners will experience a renewed excitement and enthusiasm for children's development as they experiment with how they present ordinary objects, observe how children engage with them and respond to their interests by offering further possibilities.

Observation is the key to all planning and provision, and it is hoped that the reader will observe the development of children's thinking and numeracy skills from the three standpoints of self-chosen play of the child, flexible adult-led or initiated experiences and child observation of adult everyday life activities.

Understanding how children think from a theoretical perspective

'Now, what I want is, Facts. Teach these boys and girls nothing but Facts. Facts alone are wanted in life. Plant nothing else, and root out everything else. You can only form the minds of reasoning animals upon Facts' […] The speaker, and the schoolmaster, and the third grown person present, all backed a little, and swept with their eyes the inclined plane of little vessels then and there arranged in order, ready to have imperial gallons of facts poured into them until they were full to the brim.

(Charles Dickens, Hard Times)

Learning and noticing

What makes us different from all of the animal kingdom is our capacity to think, solve problems and use mental reasoning to plan and work things out. It is our ability to reflect that enables us human beings to be so creative and inventive. White (2002) suggests that there are four characteristics of thinking.

1   It is intentional.
2   It is an activity.
3   It employs concepts.
4   It is a skill.

I would also like to add that a child needs to be able to think in order to communicate, cooperate and calculate.

Siegler and Alibali (2005: 2) describe thinking in this way:

Thinking obviously involves the higher mental processes: problem solving reasoning, creating, conceptualizing, remembering, classifying, symbolizing, planning and so on. Other examples of thinking involve more basic processes, processes at which even young children are skilled: using language, and perceiving objects and events in the external environment, to name two.

So, where does thinking begin? Maybe the most fundamental aspect of learning is noticing things, that is, making a note in our minds about the presence of something. Tiny babies are making sense of the world through all their senses, and they do this by noticing. What they are noticing is whether the sound they are hearing, the image they are seeing, the touch they are feeling or the scent they are smelling is new or familiar.

Somehow, when you notice something (especially for the first time) whether spontaneously or as a result of it being pointed out, it seems to arouse curiosity and an increased level of attention and interest. Recently I was walking in the woods and noticed an early solitary bluebell in bloom, then found myself looking at the green clumps of sprouting leaves in great detail. The more I looked, the more bluebells I saw! I then found myself examining the flowers and enjoying their exquisite detail.

Curiosity is at the heart of all learning for it leads to active enquiry. What is more, it starts in earnest the day a baby is born. You cannot make someone curious about something, but you can draw their attention to it and help them notice it.

The aim of this chapter is to focus on the theoretical background so that we can understand the basis of the EYFS framework and practice guidance with respect to the terms 'problem-solving', 'reasoning' and 'numeracy'.

Probably the two most influential theorists of the twentieth century were Piaget and Vygotsky. Piaget, in particular created a framework for understanding how children think mathematically and scientifically, and so it is worth providing a summary here.

A historical perspective

Before the twentieth century, there was little knowledge or interest in children's development of thinking skills. Babies and young children were simply viewed as empty vessels waiting to be filled by the wisdom and knowledge of their elders as illustrated in the extract from the book *Hard Times* by Charles Dickens. It did not occur to people that children could be active learners and inventors in their own right.

However, this was all to change in the 1920s and 1930s when Jean Piaget began to observe children and publish his findings. Later in the 1960s, the work of Lev Vygotsky was discovered. The two men were coincidentally born in the same year (1896), but Vygotsky died in 1934 leaving his writing and research studies undiscovered for nearly thirty years. Piaget's research, on the other hand, was recognised and published throughout his sixty years of working life until his death in 1980. What these two great thinkers had in common was that they believed that children constructed their own understanding of the world through exploration in it. However, they also differed in fundamental ways, which I shall go on to explain.

Piaget's theories of development

As a boy, Piaget had been interested in biology, which extended into a keen interest in philosophy as he became a young adult. The combination of these two interests led him on to the journey of enquiry about how knowledge might evolve, and he began to observe children. Piaget lived in an era in which Darwin's theory of evolution was relatively new, and this idea of 'development over time' influenced Piaget's theories about how children's thinking skills might evolve. Piaget's research was carried out in a systematic and structured way, from which he developed several theories, and he was particularly interested in problem-solving, reasoning and numeracy skills.

His observation methods followed a similar pattern throughout decades of research. They were as follows:

- set a child a task;
- observe the child's behaviour;
- ask the child a question (if old enough);
- analyse the child's answer.

Piaget suggested that children go through four distinct stages of development, and this idea of 'stages' has dominated developmental theories ever since. Indeed, Piaget has become known as the 'father of stage theories'. He also believed that children did not wait to have knowledge given to them; rather, they were more like little scientists who through experimenting (doing and thinking) were constructing their own meaning, understanding and reality in the world. Piaget's genius was seeing a greater intelligence beyond a baby's or toddler's limited behaviours.

Another great thinker of the time was Maria Montessori, who shared similar views to Piaget. She had a great influence on early educational practice through her work, which started by her teaching children in the slums of Italy in the early twentieth century. She, like Piaget, believed that children were independent learners, but her particular contribution was to emphasise the adults' role and responsibility to provide a stimulating and safe environment and to be guided by the children's needs and interests. With the right kind of environment, children can concentrate and learn. As Montessori wrote (1988: 249) in her vivid and passionate style: 'The child who concentrates is immensely happy; he ignores his neighbours or the visitors circulating about him. For the time being his spirit is like that of a hermit in the desert; a new consciousness has been born in him, that of his own individuality.'

Piaget's stages of development

Below is a summary of all four stages, although subsequent research has shown that children as young as three years old reach the 'concrete operational stage'.

1 **Sensorimotor Stage** (from birth to two years). Children learn through exploring the world of objects with their five senses. It is the 'doing' that stimulates curiosity and learning.

2 **Pre-Operational Stage** (from two to seven years). As children begin to learn language, they then move on and use symbols to make sense of the world, such as drawing, beginning to read and write letters and numerals. This allows them to develop more sophisticated concepts as they can remember experiences for longer periods of time.

3 **Concrete Operational Stage** (from seven to twelve years). Children can reason logically about concrete objects and events and can take another's point of view.

4 **Formal Operational Stage** (twelve years and over). Children can reason about both concrete and abstract ideas and events.

Piaget's schemas

Piaget discovered from his observations that there seemed to be general patterns of behaviour, which he described as schemas that all children use in their play. He suggested that these behavioural schemas represent 'ways of thinking' that help children to classify their experiences in order to build up their knowledge and understanding of the world. The most common schemas are:

- **rotating**: a fascination with roundness and 'rollability';
- **enveloping**: a fascination with wrapping and covering objects and themselves (including making dens);
- **transporting**: a fascination with collecting and moving objects and themselves about;
- **containing**: a fascination with filling and emptying;
- **connecting**: a fascination with fitting things together and joining themselves to things.

Stroh et al. (2008) have taken these ideas further with their theories of learning tools, which are described in Chapter 4.

How schemas work to help children progress

Piaget noticed that when children's ideas in their playful activity did not work out as planned, an impetus for more activity and new learning was created. We all know that we learn from our mistakes, but as adults we can find it uncomfortable. Children, on the other hand, enjoy the unexpected and even look out for incongruities (things that might not work).

Piaget described this 'learning when things don't work out as planned' as three processes working together in the following way. He gave them the following names:

- **Assimilation.** This is when children make sense of something new by connecting it with things they already know and fitting it in with their own way of thinking.
- **Accommodation.** This is when children adapt their way of thinking (so extending their knowledge about the world) in the light of their new experiences. The way 'assimilation' and 'accommodation' work together is through a third process that Piaget called 'equilibration'.
- **Equilibration.** This is the way children put together many bits of knowledge and create their version of the world.

- When children are happy with their thinking = this is equilibrium.
- When children become aware of their shortcomings > they become dissatisfied.
- Then children develop new modes of thought > they get rid of shortcomings.
- A new stable equilibrium is established = children are happy with their thinking.

Egocentric thinking

Piaget also believed that children below the age of seven thought about and saw the world in a qualitatively different way from adults and older children. By this I mean that he thought that young children could only see things from their own point of view and were not able to put themselves in the shoes of others. He described this as being egocentric. He also believed that children had to be 'ready' to move on to the next stage and although adults might be able to offer some guidance, they could not actually accelerate the process.

Margaret Donaldson, who was a great admirer of Piaget's ideas, questioned his assumptions about children's egocentricity and through her own research challenged some of his ideas (see Donaldson 1978). Children could see things from another's perspective from a much younger age than Piaget had found. What she discovered was that children's thinking was surprisingly sophisticated, but they often misunderstood the questions that the adults asked so gave the appearance of being egocentric. Donaldson also found that young children could be taught skills if they were actively interested in and engaged in the process. Her work has led to a wealth of further research revealing that even infants under a year old can reason (Wynn 1998, Siegler and Alibali 2005). Although some of the detail of Piaget's theories have been found to be wrong, overall they still are very important in the way they help us think about children. As Siegler (2005: 62) states:

> Piaget's theory remains a dominant force in developmental psychology, despite the fact that much of it was formulated half a century ago. Some of the reasons for its lasting appeal are the important acquisitions it describes, the large span of childhood it encompasses, and the reliability and charm of many of its observations. [...] The theory still gives us a good feel for how children think.

The relevance of Piaget's theories to EYFS practice

I have summarised here the main themes of the EYFS which come from a Piagetian perspective:

- Children are active learners and need opportunities to learn through active self-chosen play, where the children set the pace and have the time to test out ideas without external pressure.

- Children should be provided with a variety of concrete materials (everyday objects, bricks, home-corner objects, dressing-up clothes, sensory material, toy representations of the world such as animals and vehicles, etc.) to explore and experiment with in their own way.

- Adults need to observe children in order to identify their interests and respond to them. Children need to be allowed to take the lead in their learning.

- The role of the practitioner is that of a facilitator rather than a direct teacher.

- Prepared activities should be age- and stage-appropriate as children need to be 'ready' to learn from them.

- Practitioners should provide opportunities for children to be actively involved in their own planning as well as the doing of any practical experiences, whether it is creating a den, organising a game or making some biscuits.

- Children need to be valued and known as individuals for they will each be creating their own individual 'versions' of how they see the world.

Vygotsky's theories of development

Vygotsky died of tuberculosis in 1934, with his half-completed writings and experiments 'undiscovered' until 1961. His most well-known work, *Mind in Society* was first published in 1978. Since then, his inspired thinking has had a profound influence on educational theorists and educational policy-makers in the way they view the role of teachers and caregivers in children's learning.

Vygotsky, like Piaget, saw children as actively making sense of the world through their own explorations, but he differed from Piaget in that he focused his attention on how children's learning is primarily 'social'. He believed that children develop their thinking skills through shared experiences with supportive adults and older children. He believed that you could not separate learning and culture. For example, young children in Britain are fascinated by vehicles and quickly differentiate between cars, trucks, motorbikes and buses, etc., whereas children who live in the native forest communities of South America may have little knowledge of vehicles but will know from an early age which plants are poisonous and which are good for eating.

Vygotsky thought that the way in which children gain this knowledge is through language, and he saw language as a fundamental tool for thinking. He also felt that instead of children 'going through stages of development' as a natural learning process, it is the activity of learning itself that nudges children along in their development.

Even before babies learn to talk, Vygotsky believed that they were communicating through their behaviour. For example, he described pointing as babies' first 'social act' because babies not only point to reach for something, they also know that pointing will get the attention of their caregiver.

Zone of proximal development

Vygotsky created this term as a way of explaining the 'gap', as Sue Robson (2006) puts it, between what a child is able to do on their own and what 'more' they can do with some help from someone who is more advanced than them. What he noticed was that children can often reason and do more complicated tasks with help on one day, and then, with active practice, on the next day they are able to do these same tasks on their own.

This explains Vygotsky's view of why caregivers, teachers and older children play such a vital role in helping children to learn. Vygotsky also strongly suggested that children learn best through play, where the joint attention between child and adult (or older child) creates this 'zone for proximal development'. I would almost describe this zone as that marvellous place where you discover you have competence in something (when there's a helping hand) that was dangling just out of reach on your own.

Recent research (Effective Pre-School and Primary Education 3–11 Project, DfES 1997–2003) highlighted that quality conversations between children and adults, and children and children, are important in developing 'problem-solving', 'reasoning' and 'numeracy skills', which has driven current policy-making, creating the EYFS framework. Siraj-Blatchford et al. (2002) also describe how sustained shared thinking is facilitated where adults and children are jointly involved.

The philosophy behind the early educational practice in the Italian town of Reggio Emilia, described as the Reggio Approach, which has been enthusiastically embraced in many early years settings across the UK, is also based on positive relationships and dialogue between parents, children and teachers, echoing Vygotsky's theoretical standpoint.

The relevance of Vygotsky's theories to EYFS practice

I have summarised here the main themes of the EYFS that come from a Vygotskian perspective:

- Children are active learners and learn best through play.
- Collaborative thinking between adults and children, and children and children, promotes learning.
- Adults play a vital role in helping children to do tasks that they would be unable to do alone.
- Observation forms a continuous process of assessment of children's abilities, taking into account the 'zone of proximal development' as children are changing all the time.
- Language is of vital importance in enabling children to make sense of the world and develop their thinking, so adults need to listen to children.
- Language is of vital importance as a means for the adult to give knowledge and direction to children, so adults need to talk to children.
- Adult support is an essential part of learning but should be tailored to the children depending on the situation. In some cases it might be direct instruction, in others the merest hint.

The development of problem-solving, reasoning and numeracy

Problem-solving and reasoning

In normal everyday life, the word 'problem' often comes into our conversations, but the way we use it is usually to describe something that we are not comfortable with, something negative or something we want to change when it may be difficult to do so. Indeed, the word 'problem' is used as much as an adjective as it is used as a noun. For example, we might talk of problem teenagers, problem neighbours or problem teeth. We might describe things like 'my weight problem' or 'the traffic problem'. In all these instances, there is a feeling that the problem is 'out there' and we don't want it.

However, the term 'problem-solving' as used by psychologists could not be more positive! It is the very essence of human intelligence and achievement. Even before babies can walk or talk they are setting themselves problems to solve. For problem-solving is about having a goal in mind and working out how to achieve that goal. Indeed, children in their play and normal everyday life are constantly setting themselves challenges which are, in effect, difficult goals. No wonder life is so exciting! I once observed a toddler named Tom, who wanted a cup from a high shelf in the kitchen. His mother was not readily available so Tom dragged a chair towards the worktop and proceeded to clamber on to the chair. He then climbed on to the surface of the worktop, from where he could now successfully pick up his self-chosen cup. He then put the cup on to the worktop and reversed the climbing process till he was back on the floor. He could now reach the cup and looked deeply satisfied as he took it to his mother. Needless to say, the chair was not returned! We might not approve of his strategy (with our adult eyes worrying about physical danger) but we cannot deny his satisfaction at achieving his goal by himself.

This short story illustrates a key element in problem-solving, and that is planning. The planning stages are as follows:

- Having a goal. Tom wants the cup.
- Seeing an obstacle. It's out of his reach on a high shelf.
- Working out a strategy. Tom drags a chair and climbs up to the worktop.
- Achieving the goal. Tom can now reach and have his chosen cup.

In this example, there was no other way, in Tom's mind, to get the cup (without the aid of his mother) other than to work out the 'chair strategy'. In this case, it turned out to be rather a good strategy. Children under five often find it difficult to exercise the patience necessary to work out the best strategy when they want to have something and cannot stop themselves from charging straight towards the goal.

Numeracy

Over the years, there have been various terms used to describe children's development of early number skills, such as mathematical skills and arithmetic skills. In education, the term 'numeracy' is now used to cover all skills involved in carrying out arithmetic tasks. These include the practical skills of counting, measuring, calculating and puzzle-solving as well as the ability to read, write and make sense of mathematical symbols.

Simple mathematical knowledge, for children under four, arises out of self-chosen play, such as heuristic play (see Chapter 4) and the seeing and noticing of what adults do in ordinary everyday life. Children need to see adults using counting, for example, to get a 'sense' of what it is all about. More sophisticated mathematical knowledge comes from not only self-chosen play but also guidance and shared activity with adults.

In this part of the chapter, I want to look at the terms we use and what we mean by them as well as giving a theoretical basis to the understanding of children's development of counting skills.

What is number?

We use numbers all the time in our everyday lives, but what exactly are they? We know about numbers, but it is difficult to explain them. Numbers are the names we give to describe the 'sense' of oneness, twoness, threeness and so on. We use numbers to help us order our world, for counting, calculating and measuring about concrete objects or abstract ideas. Numbers help us develop concepts and ideas. Indeed, numbers can have infinite meanings and are often termed as magical.

What do we mean by counting?

Any practitioner knows that counting is one of the basic arithmetic skills that children learn. Indeed, being able to count reliably up to ten objects is one of the early learning goals of the EYFS for children by the time they reach five years of age. However, counting has two meanings, and we often muddle the two when we describe children as being able to count.

Counting is:

- reciting the number names in sequence for the simple pleasure in doing it (rote counting) – nursery rhymes are often children's first experience of this and are very important in early numeracy;
- reciting numbers as a means to enumerate, that is, to work out how many there are, in a collection of things.

Before children are thirty months old, counting is entirely a social activity, and it is not until about the age of three that children get a sense that counting is about quantity. It is only when they are about four they can begin to reliably count out a small number of things. However, research suggests that it is not until children reach about five or six years old that they are interested in getting their calculations right (Sophian 1998). It is therefore very important that children are not introduced to formal arithmetic sums until they have had the opportunity to gain a sound understanding of the concepts through playing with concrete materials.

Let me introduce you to Holly, who is two years old. This is how her parents have described some of her interest in counting and the language of numbers.

> We had two cups on the table, and Holly said she would like 'both of them'. I asked her how many cups there were, but she was rather flummoxed by this question. We were also flummoxed that she knew 'both' was for two objects but didn't seem interested in the fact there were actually two of them.

Holly refers to couples as 'you two', so Holly's father and I can be addressed as 'you two' as can both her grandparents. I think this is just a phrase to her as she couldn't explain that she's saying it because there are two people.

When I was peeling an orange recently, Holly asked me if I was 'turning the orange inside out'. When I had finished, she wanted to share out the segments, so I tried a small experiment of counting a few with her. Together we were able to count that there were five, although she couldn't give me the answer when I asked afterwards. Holly then ate one of the segments, and I asked her to count them again. With great enthusiasm, she counted to five again!

What is apparent from these dialogues is that Holly is trying out her language to see what response she gets from the adults without understanding the meaning of the numbers.

The development of children's counting skills

Gellman and Gallistel (1978) suggested that there are five counting principles that children need in order to be able to reliably count to work out quantities. The counting principles are:

1 **stable order** – knowing you recite numbers in the same pattern (even if you are not very good at it when you are two!);
2 **one-to-one correspondence** – knowing that each number pairs up to one object (you do not count the same object twice);
3 **cardinality** – knowing that the last number you say is the one that describes the whole set;
4 **object order irrelevance** – knowing that you can count objects in any order (see Piaget anecdotal story below);
5 **abstraction** – knowing that all kinds of things can be counted.

Piaget tells an anecdote (1973: 81), which clearly illustrates the order irrelevance principle:

A friend of mine […] when he was about 4 or 5 years old […] started to amuse himself by placing some pebbles in a straight line and counting them, for example one to ten from left to right. After this he counted them from right to left and to his great surprise he still found ten. He then put them in a circle and, with enthusiasm, counted them – again ten so he counted them in the opposite direction and he found there were ten in both directions. He went on arranging the pebbles in all sorts of ways and finished by convincing himself that the sum, ten, was independent of the order of the pebbles.

We need to note the age (four to five years) at which Piaget's friend was playing with these pebbles and thinking about the numbers in this way. How often do we assume that much younger children already understand order irrelevance, simply because they are competent rote counters?

Numbers as symbols

A symbol is a mark, drawing, sound, object, etc., that stands for something else, and number symbols are called numerals. I have already described that rote-counting happens before children understand that the numbers are for working out 'how many'. In the same way, the act of counting for calculation happens before a child makes any sense of how to use numerals. Children from about the age of three or four like to recognise numerals and take great delight in noticing things such as television channel numbers, car-registration numbers, numbers on a calendar, birthday cards and clocks to name but a few. However, they do not know what they are 'for'. They have not yet developed the concepts to 'work with' numerals.

It is therefore very important that children are given plenty of opportunity to play with ordinary and everyday objects to develop their number concepts. There has been great concern expressed by those in early education that children are being 'put off' maths or find 'maths difficult' because they are being introduced to formal or symbolic mathematical sums too soon.

Baratta-Lorton (1998: xiv) expresses this very clearly at the beginning of the book describing her *Mathematics Their Way* programme:

A page of abstract symbols, no matter how carefully designed or simplified, because of its very nature, cannot involve the child's senses the way real materials can. Symbols are not the concept, they are only a representation of the concept, and as such are abstractions describing something which is not visible to the child. Real materials, on the other hand, can be manipulated to illustrate the concept concretely and can be experienced visually by the child.

Why use ordinary and everyday materials?

Children in group childcare or in early education settings are becoming increasingly immersed in manufactured and plastic toys, and this is particularly the case for babies and toddlers under two years of age. Whilst these toys might be entertaining, their value is often transitory or fleeting. For older children, the catalogues tempt practitioners to spend a lot of money on what are described as 'educational materials' whose value is either limited or in which the children quickly lose interest. Manufactured toys and educational materials cost a lot of money too. However, when children are able to play with natural and household materials, it engages them in much more satisfying and meaningful ways and allows for much more in-depth problem-solving and learning through their own interests.

Why sing nursery rhymes?

Many nursery rhymes are about numbers and counting. Have you ever wondered why? The whole rhythm and beat of nursery rhymes are a baby's and young child's first experience of music. Music is about counting the beat and playing around with sounds. It is about putting sounds in sequences and pairs and adding and subtracting them. Music is number in sound. No wonder many of the words or themes in nursery rhymes contain numbers and counting. What is more, babies and young children have a fascination with their own bodies, so pointing to 'one nose', 'two eyes', 'five fingers' and 'ten toes' provides the first meaningful context for the number words.

The tradition of singing nursery rhymes to babies and children is a worldwide phenomenon in urban and rural communities whether technologically advanced or not. It is also a cultural tradition in all cultures that has gone on for thousands of years, predating writing and printing. It is a tradition that is in danger of dying out in our 'rush' to teach children skills. Nursery rhymes should be a source of joy at the heart of every intimate relationship between a child and caregiver, whether that caregiver is a parent, teacher, childminder or early years practitioner.

Nursery rhymes

Sing nursery rhymes at intimate times, for babies find the experience both soothing and stimulating, and it is a wonderful way to play with number language and have fun. I shall offer a nursery rhyme in many of the 'activities' sections throughout Chapters 6, 7 and 8. However, the rhymes are relevant for all ages and all aspects of number development. So you can pick and choose from any of these rhymes for any of the children, whatever age you are working with.

Round and Round the Garden

Round and round the garden
Like a teddy bear;
One step, two step,
Tickle you under there!

The role of the early years practitioner and the EYFS

A critical look at the EYFS

In Chapter 1, I presented a historical overview of Piaget's and Vygotsky's theories about how children learn and develop with a particular focus on problem-solving and numeracy skills. It is important to understand their complementary theoretical standpoints to be able to make sense of the EYFS because the framework and practice guidance draw upon a blend of both their views.

In a sense, the EYFS is rather Piagetian with its focus on early learning goals and dividing up children's development by age. Piaget's approach is seductive because the ideas of 'stages and schemas' create neat categories so that we can conceptualise development more easily. It implies that children go through precise stages of development, and, whilst there is a recognition that children develop at different rates and in different ways, a newcomer to the subject might feel children should be doing certain things at certain times. There is also the danger of 'compartmentalising' learning, when in reality there is such overlap when children are actually playing. It would be a shame if practitioners' enjoyment of observation and getting to know their key children was spoilt because they were worrying about which 'boxes to tick' in the six areas of development.

The EYFS is also Vygotskyian because throughout the framework and practice-guidance documents there is reference to 'how' practitioners can support children in their learning, from being suitably trained to encouraging children to notice things or to be engaged in certain types of activities. It appeals to our natural sociability and wanting to feel part of a community and culture. It is excellent that the EYFS places an emphasis on helping children feel safe and secure through warm and loving relationships with their key persons. Indeed, learning can only happen in the context of such relationships as I have described in my book on early play (Hughes 2006).

The tension between childcare and education

There is an unspoken tension between the principles of childcare and the principles of education, which is largely not thought about or understood but which can contribute to misunderstandings about the role of the caregiver or teacher. This is particularly so as professionals are trying to make sense of and implement the EYFS.

The language in the framework and practice-guidance documents blends the principles of caring and teaching, which is excellent at one level but can lead to anxiety for those working in the field who feel unsure about their role. Are they supposed to be teaching children or caring for them? How do these two notions work in harmony together? There has been common agreement for the past thirty years between both teachers and childcare workers (nursery nurses, childminders, etc.) that children learn through play. However, the role of the adult in that process has often looked very different.

The traditional principles of childcare have been, as the name suggests, caring for children. This has meant making sure that very young children are physically and emotionally safe and secure. Elinor Goldschmied's innovative idea of the key-person approach (Goldschmied et al. 2003) is now a key feature of the EYFS framework and brings the caring role firmly into the realm of education.

The traditional principles of education have been to provide stimulating activities and materials for children and to guide them in their learning. In order to do this, teachers have studied how children learn to inform their practice. The EYFS practice guidance offers a clear picture of children's development in the six identified areas to guide and support all practitioners in their educational role.

The importance of encouragement

I have noticed there is much reference to the word 'encourage' (on the part of practitioners) in the 'effective practice' and 'planning and resourcing' sections of the EYFS practice guidance. The *Collins English Dictionary* definition of the word 'encourage' is as follows:

- To give (someone) the confidence to do something.
- To stimulate someone by approval or help.

The word also suggests giving someone else the 'courage' to do something. I feel it is worth reflecting upon what this word means as it underpins one's interpretation of how 'involved' an adult is in a child's play and learning.

When babies and young children feel safe and secure, they need no encouragement as such. It is their natural instinct to want to play and socialise. Babies and very young children only need encouragement when they are anxious or timid and are feeling insecure. It is therefore important to work on one's relationship with an anxious child first. This means giving the child your attention or simply giving the child the time to be able to watch you or other children do things. It means letting the child know you are there for them and care about them and, very importantly, will not rush them.

When encouragement feels like pressure

Encouragement can feel like pressure when there is a deadline involved. Let us reflect upon our own experience. Maybe you want help choosing clothes for a holiday, but your friend tells you that she is only free on the afternoon before you leave. Suddenly the pleasure of a shopping trip turns into a 'route march' round the town.

Similarly, it is easy to inadvertently put children under pressure, when they have to fit in with our 'planned activities' or when we 'take over' a child's interest. I recently visited a nursery where a group of four-year-old children were making 'Mother's Day' cards. The children were shown the various materials they could choose from to make their creations. One of the practitioners could see that a girl needed some help but offered it before the child asked for it. From that point, although this girl 'went along' with what the adult suggested, the pleasure had clearly gone. The creative impulse had changed into a feeling of 'oughts' and 'shoulds'.

If you notice babies or children doing something that may need some assistance and feel you ought to point it out or give help, the babies or children might feel they ought to be interested or to do as you suggest. The play and learning experience becomes imbued with pleasing the adults, and children are excellent in going along with what they think the adults want of them.

We all notice the moment of individual will when a child says 'no', and it makes us feel threatened or irritated. However, do we notice when we are exerting our will and when children play 'our game' or copy what we do to keep us happy?

It is therefore important to be attentive and sensitive to the children whenever you feel the urge to encourage and decide whether or not you would be intrusive and interfering. In essence, young children need no encouragement in their play.

The role of the early years practitioner

With these thoughts about encouragement in mind, these are the main aspects of the adult's role in an early years setting:

- to offer a secure and loving relationship to each key child;
- to share in a child's pleasure and to be responsive to their emotions and play interests;
- to be unobtrusive when children are concentrating in their play;
- to follow the children's lead in what interests and excites them;
- to offer guidance only when it is asked for;
- to sensitively encourage children when they are timid but want to participate;
- to provide a clean, appealing and well-resourced environment, both inside and out, so the children have plenty of choice and can see and access what they are choosing to play with;
- to make sure that play equipment is in good condition;
- to plan ahead so that a variety of play opportunities are available (such as permission forms for a visit to the park or ingredients for a cooking session);
- to share with parents what the children are doing, learning and how they are feeling.

It is important for practitioners to develop secure and positive relationships with the parents as well as with their children.

Learning tools and heuristic play

I hear and I forget,
I see and I remember,
I do and I understand.
                    (Confucius)

In this chapter, I want to introduce a new and valuable theoretical model, 'learning tools', that will help practitioners to understand how children are learning number concepts in their play. I will then describe 'heuristic play', which starts in toddlerhood and is the foundation of all problem-solving and number-skills learning.

What are concepts?

Concepts are objects, ideas and experiences grouped together on the basis of their similarity. Some examples of the most common concepts are those of time, space, living things and number. The way we create concepts is by categorising. What is fascinating is the fact that there are infinite ways in which objects and events can be categorised. An adult's idea of how a collection of objects might be categorised could be very different from a child's. We might want to categorise a collection of objects according to their colour such as whether they are 'red', whereas a child might find it much more interesting to categorise them according to their textural quality such as whether or not they are 'squashy'! Here, colour and textural feel are concepts. Here are some thoughts about concepts:

- Concepts help us to simplify the world.

- Concepts allow us to organise our experience into coherent patterns.

- Concepts allow us to draw inferences in situations where we may not have had direct experience.

- Concepts save us mental effort because we can use previous knowledge to help us with new circumstances.

Let us briefly consider the early concept of time. We know that children like routine because it gives them a sense of security. It also means they can predict what is going to happen. Routine events punctuate time, allowing children to gain their first sense of past, present and future as well as the idea of the passage of time.

As children get a bit older and become familiar with numbers and their own age, they can play around with the idea of time even more. This can be illustrated by four-year-old Emma's comments as recounted by her mother. (Emma has an older brother, Francesco who is six.)

> Playing with the age gap between herself and Francesco is another frequent speculation. She will make up possible future scenarios always maintaining the two-year gap. For example, she said, 'When I am twenty-five I want to be a doctor and Francesco, who will be twenty-seven will be a teacher. But he will become a teacher before I become a doctor. But I won't go to school for longer, because I start school two years later.

As Emma has sophisticated language skills, she can begin to explore mathematical ideas verbally and does not need to rely entirely on concrete experiences or objects to think about the concepts of time and numbers. However, in the first three years of life, numbers are only meaningful to babies and children when they are using their senses to experiment with concrete objects.

The concept of number is mankind's way of making the vastness of this world manageable in the mind. Numbers help us when we put things in categories and make calculations and measurements, and they allow us to write complicated ideas in a shorthand way.

Learning tools

In the earlier chapters, I described some well-known theoretical models that have been used to help us understand how children develop their thinking and learning skills. I would now like to introduce a new way of understanding how children learn to make sense of the world. It is the idea of learning tools, upon which Katrin Stroh and Thelma Robinson base their therapeutic practice (functional learning) with developmentally delayed children (Stroh et al. 2008).

A tool is an implement that we use with our hands to help us do a particular type of work or task. A wooden spoon enables us to stir hot food in a saucepan so that it cooks evenly and does not stick to the pan. A pen enables us to communicate ideas or instructions in a written format. Learning tools are 'mental tools' used by all children in all cultures to help them learn and to solve problems. The first and most basic learning tool is 'placing', which is the ability to pick objects up and to put them down in another place. Without the ability to intentionally move things about we could never be creative or manage even the simplest task in our everyday lives.

The development of learning tools is a natural part of a child's normal development like the learning of language skills. However, children need to be given the opportunity to use the learning tools in their play in order to become competent thinkers and problem solvers. In Chapters 6, 7 and 8, I will be describing plenty of play material and activities which promote these learning tools.

The learning tools as identified by Stroh and Robinson are as follows:

- **Placing.** This is filling a space with an object which means moving it from one place to another.
- **Banging.** This means holding an object and bringing it into contact with another object or surface. At first, babies only use one hand, but later they will either bring two objects together (such as banging together two bricks) or use two separate objects to bang on another object (such as using two sticks to bang a drum). Banging with two hands integrates neural connections between both sides of the brain.
- **Piling.** This is placing objects one on top of the other to make a pile. This then leads to the ability to make towers and structures with bricks. The importance of this learning tool is that it enables a child to have an idea in mind (to create a mental image) before actually creating something concrete.

- **Pairing.** This means noticing that two objects are identical and then bringing them together. As toddlers first discover that different objects can be alike, it leads to activity that promotes the ability to hold something in mind whilst searching for its identical match.

- **Matching.** This is comparing and contrasting one image or object with another that is either identical or similar. As children begin to learn the function of different objects, for example, this learning tool allows the ability to select and make choices such as putting cutlery into the different sections of a cutlery drawer.

- **Sorting**. This means recognising that objects or images which are the same or similar can be grouped together in sets of more than two. This is an extension of the pairing and matching learning tools. This requires mental flexibility, as sorting into sets is about recognising attributes, making choices and is the basis of classification. It is important for children to develop the ability to 'sort out' their world in order to feel safe, such as identifying people into family, friends and strangers or that all things on wheels can move along the ground. The importance of sorting and classifying in children's mathematical development is critical.

- **Sequencing.** This means carrying out a series of actions one after the other. In this way, a child learns to continue actions in a smooth and ongoing manner. This sequencing activity allows a child to arrange and order things and to anticipate and predict what is to come. It is the basis of problem-solving and reasoning skills.

Heuristic play

This term was first used in the 1980s when Elinor Goldschmied, Gwen Macmichael and I were conducting research into the play of toddlers (Goldschmied and Jackson 2003, Hughes 2006). The name 'heuristic play' comes from the Greek word *eurisko,* which means 'I discover' or 'I find and understand.' When Archimedes in the ancient tale is said to have jumped out of his bath shouting 'Eureka!' having discovered the law of the displacement of water, he made a discovery from the observation of his actions. In the same way, toddlers are constantly making discoveries about the properties of objects through the actions of their experimental play of filling and emptying, banging, throwing, etc. Indeed, from toddlerhood, children are developing their learning tools from picking up objects and wondering, 'What can I do with it?' Toddlers and young children are interested not only in objects but also in their own bodies, tirelessly experimenting with climbing, balancing, rolling, fitting in small places, etc.

The most significant things about heuristic play are that it is self-chosen, experimental and non-social. Non-social means that children play with the material because they are interested in how that material can be manipulated. Children may copy an adult or another child. However, the play demands concentration and focus, which social interaction with others would interrupt. It is therefore very important for the adult to sit nearby (having set out a range of material attractively) and be responsive but not intrusive. Indeed, it is best to stay quiet and simply be peaceful and comfortable to allow a small group of children to concentrate without the fear of interruption or distraction.

Some typical behaviour that can be described as heuristic play is as follows:

- picking up objects and putting them in different places;
- putting objects in containers such as tins, boxes, tubes and trolleys;
- emptying objects out of containers;
- piling objects into towers and knocking them down;
- rolling objects along the floor;
- sliding objects through tubes or down sloping surfaces;
- slotting small objects inside larger objects;
- lining up objects;
- shaking or banging objects together;
- collecting similar or identical objects and putting them in containers or in heaps;
- putting rings on rods, posts, handlebars, etc.;
- spinning cylindrical or round-shaped objects;
- dropping objects from a height;
- screwing or unscrewing lids;
- squeezing objects in fists or between fingers and thumb;
- looking inside or through objects;
- draping ribbons, scarves and chains around their necks.

Some number concepts learnt through heuristic play

When toddlers play with objects and containers, they are learning concepts fundamental to numeracy even before they have the language to give a name to them. Indeed, as the quote by Confucius on p. 25 aptly illustrates, it is not until we actually try something out that we really understand it.

Here are some concepts that toddlers from the age of about ten months are learning through heuristic play:

- same and different;
- little and big;
- little fits inside big but not the other way round;
- longness and shortness;
- one, few and many;
- heavy and light;
- addition and subtraction.

In the following chapters you will be offered suggestions of play material that promotes heuristic play. This kind of play is the forerunner of all intellectual thinking and accelerates the development of learning tools.

When children develop language, their play becomes more imaginative, and they are able to play with others in a more cooperative way as they can share their ideas and negotiate, which leads to extended problem-solving activity.

Putting the principles of the EYFS into practice

The principles of the EYFS which guide the work of early years practitioners are grouped into four themes. I shall state these themes and explain how they work together to underpin effective practice in the delivery of the EYFS. This will be particularly related to the area of learning and development, problem-solving, reasoning and numeracy.

A unique child

> Every child is a competent learner from birth who can be resilient, capable, confident and self assured.
>
> (DfES 2007b: 5)

This principle highlights a child's natural ability to learn. Throughout the next three chapters I have given examples of what children have said and done in their spontaneous play to illustrate this. Even babies of under six months old are actively using their senses to discriminate between what they can recognise and what is unfamiliar. When children are trusted to take safe risks in their play, they learn to think. When children think, they take care and learn skills. When children learn skills, they become resilient, capable, confident and self-assured.

Positive relationships

> Children learn to be strong and independent from a base of loving and secure relationships with parents or a key person.
>
> (DfES 2007b: 5)

Every baby and child needs love in order to thrive, and a secure loving relationship is the foundation for all successful learning. We all have to manage the balance between anxiety and curiosity when we are learning something new. It is what drives us all in our learning. However, when anxiety becomes overwhelming, we become frozen with fear and are unable to do anything. When babies and children first come to a setting, whether it is in the home of a childminder, a day-care nursery, a pre-school or a nursery class, they will be feeling frightened and insecure. The most important thing is to help the baby or child settle in with his or her key person. This may take a long time for some children. It does not matter. The time making positive relationships will lead the way to successful learning and happy children.

In the next three chapters, I refer to the practitioner's role as a 'facilitating' one, which means 'easing the way' in a child's learning. A baby feels secure if you are sitting comfortably nearby when he or she is playing with a treasure basket. Small children will take delight in collecting pebbles or conkers on a walk knowing their key person is with them sharing in their delight. Children learn problem-solving and number skills through their efforts to help their key person in tasks such as setting the table and sharing out food.

Enabling environments

> The environment plays a key role in supporting and extending children's development and learning.
>
> (DfES 2007b: 5)

This principle reminds practitioners of their responsibility to create a safe, stimulating and varied environment for the children in their care. A vital role of the adults is to provide the props to aid children's learning and extend their play opportunities and fun.

In the next part of this book, I have provided many ideas to help you, the reader, feel confident in what you already provide as well as hopefully inspiring you to try out new materials and activities. The emphasis of this book has been on using natural and everyday materials for the children to play with. Children are being limited if they are only offered plastic toys and commercially produced games. There is far more scope for problem-solving and the development of mathematical skills when children are allowed to experiment with open-ended material which can be found within the home or in the natural world.

Learning and development

Children develop and learn in different ways and at different rates, and all areas of learning and development are equally important and interconnected.

(DfES 2007b: 5)

This principle encourages creativity for both children and practitioners. It is important for practitioners (especially for those working in a team) to embrace their different interests and talents in being creative about how to use materials to support children in their learning and development of mathematical skills.

Singing rhymes, playing music and telling stories are ways to engage with the world of number through rhythm, noise, imagination, intimacy and social interaction. Providing a rich variety of objects for the treasure basket, heuristic play, sorting, matching and counting allows children to use all their senses and to develop thinking and concentration skills. Using household material in the outside play area allows children to develop their motor skills and to experiment with calculation, shape and measures. Allowing children to assist in routine tasks builds trust, skills and self-confidence at their own rate and in their own way. It also helps children to develop social-communication skills.

I feel it is important to make clear that the age bands used in the next three chapters are only for general guidance purposes and in no way imply that children 'should' be doing particular things at a particular age. This principle states this idea clearly. It is worth trying out the use of various materials and observing the children to see whether they show interest or not and take the lead from them.

It is also a feature of very young children that family circumstances, such as the birth of a new baby and parental separation or illness can affect their play and development. At such times, when children are under more stress than usual, they may choose to seek more comfort from the adults than want to play energetically or explore. Also, they may want to revert to a 'younger' type of play. Similarly, children can spontaneously choose to step back to a level of activity where they were comfortable at an earlier time followed by a leap forward in their development shortly afterwards.

Throughout the book I have offered a range of different play-opportunity ideas, which will hopefully appeal to all children from birth to sixty months in their different areas of learning, but with the particular focus on problem-solving, reasoning and numeracy.

6 Numbers as labels and for counting

From birth–11 months

What children have said or done

This is an observation of a seven-month-old baby playing with objects in the
treasure basket and experiencing the different textures of two particular objects.
This baby is too young to be able to deliberately pick up and release objects
at will. The baby feels safe and secure in the presence of her key person.

Alice is sitting beside the treasure basket with her key person, Lesley,
who is sitting nearby on a comfortable low chair. The atmosphere is
calm and quiet. After Alice has seen that Lesley is no longer moving
about but is settled on the chair, she pays no attention to her as she
looks at the objects in the basket. She reaches out with one arm, and

her fingers touch a garlic press. Instantly, her fingers grasp one of the handles, and she pulls the object out of the basket. The other handle drops down as Alice tries to bring the one she is holding to her mouth. She licks the handle as her other hand brushes the leather strap of a tiny handbag. Still holding the garlic press in the first hand, that arm drops as her attention is now drawn to the leather bag. She curls her fingers around the strap and tugs lightly but the bag is stuck. She has forgotten the garlic press although she is still tightly gripping the handle. As she tugs more at the leather strap, she lets go of the garlic press and begins to chew on the leather, still only using one hand.

Look, listen and note

Babies under nine months old usually use one hand at a time when playing with objects. Observe the babies in your care and see when they begin to use both hands together and when they are able to choose when and how to pick up and release objects.

Activities, objects and rhymes

Gazing

One of the most important things a baby likes to do is gaze at things. A large part of a baby's day will be spent gazing, and through this babies are noticing patterns and changes in their lives. Babies love to gaze at:

● abstract patterns (such as friezes around the cot or changing mat);

● other children at play;

● adults doing everyday tasks.

Treasure basket

At around four to five months babies begin to reach for objects and put them in their mouths. This is a baby's first experience of playing with objects. Adults do not need to directly encourage play in babies, for this

Treasure basket

comes out of natural curiosity. However, adults need to provide stimulating play material to arouse that curiosity. The ideal play material for a
baby from about four to ten months (who is sitting and not yet crawling)
is a treasure basket. This is a round sturdy basket filled with eighty to
100 natural and everyday objects, which a baby can pick up, mouth
and examine. It offers a baby the opportunity to make choices, such as
'which' object to select and 'whether' or 'when' to pick up an object.

Below is a quote from my book on early play about why it is important
to offer a baby the opportunity to make choices.

> Choice implies selection, variety and possibility. Variety implies
> characteristics and description. By being able to select, one is not
> only embracing variety, but there is also the choice to 'act' rather
> than simply 'react' to desires and impulses. The ability to select
> has become a fundamental requirement in this day and age and
> underpins all decision making. Being able to make decisions in
> a world of choices is the gateway to being in control of one's life.
>
> (Hughes 2006: 32)

Offering the treasure basket

Create a quiet time (preferably thirty to forty-five minutes), without inter-ruption, to offer the treasure basket to a baby who is at the mouthing stage. The adult needs to sit in a comfortable chair and be quiet, attentive and responsive to the baby. It is important not to be intrusive. Notice what the baby is playing with. Is the baby spending a long time with one object? Maybe today the baby is working his or her way through the pile of objects as if searching for a particular one? Is the baby absorbed in the play or is the baby distracted by others? Is the baby copying another baby? Your enjoyment of this peaceful time will create the right atmosphere that encourages concentration and pleasure in the baby.

Materials needed

- Treasure basket: wicker (rigid), 12 centimetres high, 30–35 centi-metres in diameter, flat-bottomed and no handles.

- 80–100 different objects.

Some ideas for treasure-basket objects

Natural objects

- shells (various types)

- pine cone

- loofah

- large pebbles (various shapes)

- pumice stone

- sheepskin (10 by 5 centimetres)

- coconut shell

- a lemon and an orange

- sponge

- piece of fur (10 by 5 centimetres)

- piece of driftwood

- gourd.

Objects made from wood

- curtain ring
- spoons (various) and spatula
- coaster
- door wedge
- block
- bracelet
- napkin ring
- egg cup
- egg
- ball
- light pull
- dolly peg
- empty salt or pepper cellar
- small turned bowl.

Objects made from metal

- bunch of keys
- bangle
- egg cup
- curtain ring
- napkin ring
- egg poacher cup
- drawer handle
- spoons (various)
- tea strainer or sieve
- whisk
- powder compact (securely closed with superglue)

- bath chain with plug

- metal dish or bowl (smooth edged)

- chains of various weights from hardware shop

- nutcracker

- lids (different sizes)

- candle holder

- lemon squeezer

- key rings linked (10–20)

- bell

- set of measuring spoons on ring

- reindeer-type bells.

Objects made from leather and textile

- leather wallet, purse or spectacle case

- fabric wallet, purse or spectacle case

- coloured ribbons

- leather key ring

- bags of scented herbs such as lavender

- piece of flannel and other fabric offcuts (12 by 8 centimetres)

- bean bag

- juggling ball

- small teddy bear or other soft toy

Objects made from rubber

- ball

- large 'all size' plug for basin or bath

- large eraser

- coaster

- soap holder

- slip mat

- door stop.

Objects with bristles

- paintbrush (small)

- pastry brush

- bottle brush (various sizes)

- shaving brush

- toothbrush

- small shoe brush

- nailbrush

- make-up brush.

Baby with treasure basket I

Objects made from thick glass and marble

- egg
- incense-stick holder
- ornament
- vanilla-essence bottle
- lid (e.g., decanter)
- place-name holder (IKEA)
- small mirror (for make-up).

Objects manufactured from other materials

- hair roller
- woollen pom-pom balls (different sizes and colours)
- golf ball
- cane bag handle
- raffia mat

Baby with treasure basket II

- small ceramic pot

- champagne cork

- small basket

- large buttons (5 centimetres)

- string of beads on a shoelace securely tied.

Effective practice

- It is very important to make sure that you choose an uninterrupted period of the day to offer the treasure basket to a baby, so that the atmosphere is calm and the baby feels safe and secure.

- The practitioner needs to sit by the baby (or small group of babies) on a comfortable low chair in order to be able to be responsive and attentive.

Planning and resourcing

- Make sure that your treasure basket has rigid sides and is low enough and small enough for babies to reach and pick out the objects of their choice.

- The objects need to be small enough for a baby to pick up but large enough to prevent choking. It is also important to keep objects clean by regularly washing them in soap and hot water. (Avoid using chemicals for cleaning the objects.) It is also important to throw away objects which have become tatty or damaged and replace them with new ones.

- Make sure the objects are 'safe'. For example, a broken shell can suddenly have a lethally sharp edge, but whole shells are a wonderful item for exploration.

Home links

- It is a good idea for practitioners to tell parents about the treasure basket before a baby begins at a setting. Parents often need reassurance and explanation about the safety and suitability of objects in a basket.

- Invite a new parent to share in a session to observe how the babies are absorbed in their play and how the key-person adults attend to their safety, care and enjoyment.

Additional resources

- Treasure baskets can be made to order from P. H. Coate and Son, www.coates-willowbasket.co.uk. Treasure-basket sets can be ordered from Early Excellence, www.earlyexcellence.com.

- Hughes, A. M. (2006) *Developing Play for the Under 3s: The Treasure Basket and Heuristic Play,* London: David Fulton Publishers.

- Williams, S. (1983) *Round and Round the Garden: Play Rhymes for Young Children,* Oxford: Oxford University Press.

From 10–20 months

Development matters

- Develop an awareness of number games through babies' enjoyment of action rhymes and songs that relate to their experience of numbers.
- Enjoy finding their nose, eyes or tummy as part of naming games.

Key words

heuristic play, enjoyment of rhymes

43

What children have said or done

This is an observation I made of children discovering how two objects can have a relationship through exploration during heuristic play. It is also interesting how the children, although playing separately, nevertheless get ideas from and copy each other.

> Sophie is playing alongside Tom. They are both twelve months old and are enjoying a heuristic-play session. Today they are playing with curtain rings and bracelets, corks, ribbons, assorted tins and a set of twenty paper cups. Tom begins to line up the bracelets, then the line turns into more of a circle all around him. Sophie picks up a cup and puts it down. It lands inside one of the bracelets. Tom sees this and also picks up a cup then places it inside another of the bracelets. Tom repeats this until all the spaces inside the bracelets are filled. Sophie picks up one of the cups and puts it inside another cup, giggling as it slides in. She then tries to pull it out but it sticks. She finds another cup instead and puts that inside. Tom picks up one of his cups, places it in an empty tin and begins shaking it. The cup falls out. The play with these items continues for another twenty minutes.

Look, listen and note

- Notice how long children can play with open-ended materials such as containers and objects. It will surprise you!

- Notice how the children are quiet, purposeful and fully engaged when they are involved in heuristic play.

- Heuristic play is 'non-social' play, which means that the adults do not join in. However, it is important to be responsive and attentive to the children as they may want to show you something or want your help with holding an object, for example.

Activities, objects and rhymes

Heuristic play

At this age, children become fascinated by concrete objects and containers. Their play activity is purposeful and deeply absorbing as they are experimenting to see what happens. This experimental play is called Heuristic Play (see Chapter 4, pp. 28–30).

Promoting heuristic play

It is really important to provide toddlers with:

● protected physical space (for example a designated carpeted area or quiet corner) in which to attractively lay out a variety of objects and containers;

● peaceful and uninterrupted time to engage in purposeful self-chosen heuristic play (ideally, this is forty minutes, to include ten minutes of clearing up with the toddlers);

● the adult's responsive attention, making sure that the toddlers have enough play material to avoid conflict and are reassured if nervous or feeling insecure.

Also, it is important to make sure the play material is sensitively kept together during a play session, otherwise it can become a chaotic and unattractive mess very quickly. There is an art to this as you do not want to interfere with the children's own discoveries!

Suggested materials to promote heuristic play

Containers

● biscuit or whisky tins without lids on

● various sized tins with smooth rims (coffee, baby milk, etc.)

● wide-necked plastic bottles

● yoghurt pots or jars

● glass jars (tiny ones with thick glass)

- flower pots

- nesting 'alibaba' baskets

- cardboard or wooden boxes (with or without lids)

- cardboard tubes (e.g., Pringles)

- paper or plastic cups

- ice-cube trays

- purses and wallets

- small ladles.

Objects for placing and pairing

- cardboard cylinders (e.g., insides of kitchen paper, cling film or foil)

- metre lengths of silk or velvet ribbon or lace

- sanded wooden 'offcuts' from a carpenter

- bunches of keys

- metal jar lids of all sizes (jam, pickle, coffee, etc.)

- wine and champagne bottle corks (large)

- pine cones and shells

- very large buttons (5-centimetre diameter)

- different sized metal or wooden spoons

- curtain rings (wooden and metal)

- rubber door wedges

- wooden dolly pegs (smooth)

- lengths of bath chain (some 50 centimetres, some 1 metre)

- key ring links (ten links make a long enough chain)

- round wooden doorknobs

- simple and easy to handle wooden or plastic 'men' (without moving parts)

- small-wheeled wooden vehicles.

Toddlers playing with heuristic-play materials I

Objects for piling

- kitchen-roll holders with bracelets and curtain rings

- wooden mug trees

- wooden bricks of various sizes

- small boxes of various sizes

- set of nesting coasters

- Velcro hair rollers.

Toddler playing with heuristic-play materials II

Objects to roll and bounce

- pom-poms

- rubber balls

- ping pong balls

- wooden balls

- foam balls

- cotton reels

- hair rollers

- electrical cable spools (empty)

- tubes (plastic or cardboard).

Posting objects

● shoe box with hole in lid and set of balls

● boxes with slits in lids plus large buttons or small lids

● tins with holes in lid (for example from IKEA for tea lights) with drinking straws.

Slotting objects

● rubber or wooden CD storage and square coasters or CDs

● money boxes (minus bottoms) and large buttons

● several cardboard or plastic tubes with slight difference in diameter

● several hair-rollers of different sizes (to slot inside each other).

 Nursery rhyme

Clap Your Hands

Clap your hands, clap your hands,
Clap them just like me.
Touch your shoulders, touch your shoulders,
Touch them just like me,
Tap your knees, tap your knees,
Tap them just like me.
Shake your head, shake your head,
Shake it just like me.
Clap your hands, clap your hands,
Then let them quiet be.

Effective practice

It is important to organise a heuristic-play session every day if possible. Make sure that you choose a quiet and 'contained' area for this kind of play so the children feel safe that they are not going to be interrupted and so can concentrate and enjoy their play in peace.

49

Planning and resourcing

You will need to make several collections of objects (ten to fifteen types would be excellent) such as those suggested in the previous section. Make sure these objects are in good condition so they are safe for toddlers to play with. It is a good idea to store the objects in drawstring bags. A cleared space (with no other play material) is necessary for a heuristic-play session.

Home links

- Encourage parents to sing nursery rhymes by inviting them to join you when you are singing in your setting. Type up and print the words of the nursery rhymes you are using, so the parents can sing them at home.

- Parents may not be aware of heuristic play or the value of providing ordinary objects for children to play with. (However, most parents will tell you that their children, given half a chance, like to play with pans and wooden spoons in the kitchen!) Invite parents to come and join you for a heuristic-play session so they can see for themselves how the children are learning and getting pleasure from this kind of play.

- Ask parents to help you with collecting objects by giving them a list of ideas. It will not only help you in your setting but will also inspire them to make their own collections at home.

Additional resources

- Channon, J. (2005) *Teddy Jumps: Songs for the Very Young,* www.kidsmusiceducation.com.

- Goldschmied, E. and Hughes, A. M. (1992) *Heuristic Play with Objects,* London: National Children's Bureau (film on DVD).

From 16–36 months

Development matters

- Say some counting words randomly.

- Distinguish between quantities, recognising that a group of objects is more than one.

- Gain awareness of one-to-one correspondence through categorising belongings, starting with 'mine' or 'Mummy's'.

- Have some understanding of one and two, especially when the number is important for them.

- Create and experiment with symbols and marks.

- Use some number language such as 'more' and 'a lot'.

- Recite some number names in sequence.

Key words

first counting, recognising more than one

What children have said and done

This is what key person Sally described of Paul (nineteen months) to his parents, which vividly illustrates this stage of development.

Paul has become really excited about noticing things that are the same and similar, and if he sees two things together, he says 'dee dor' and his arms and legs go rigid with excitement. This 'dee dor' seems to mean 'lots' to him. Here are some examples of things he has noticed and responded to:

- two baby lotion bottles
- two sandwiches
- two nappies
- two bikes close together

- two socks
- two cups
- two lorries side by side on the roadside (when on a local walk).

I really enjoy his excitement and interest, which seems to make him do it all the more!

Look, listen and note

Children are developing language rapidly at this stage, and it is important to 'tune in' to what they are telling you so there is a shared pleasure in their discoveries.

Notice how children will copy the number language you use but without necessarily 'understanding' what the words mean. (For example, Holly, at twenty-six months often referred to her parents as 'you two', but did not understand the concept of two.)

Activities, objects and rhymes

Watching and copying

Children of this age are extremely interested to see what adults and older children are doing. They will watch attentively on one day and, even without being shown, will try to do what they have seen. For example, if an older child piles up some bricks and counts them, a rising two-year-old will copy this and issue a 'chanting' sound like counting.

Take any opportunity to count aloud in your everyday activity, such as pouring out drinks, helping to put on shoes, putting out cushions to sit on so children hear the counting words and seeing your actions that go with the words.

If children watch you setting a table, then it is likely they will try doing the same in the role-play area if you have plates, spoons, etc. You might like to let children 'help' you if they are interested.

You will probably find that not only do children like to fill and empty containers, they increasingly like to move things about – the bigger the better! (This is the placing tool in action.) Through the action of moving things about, they discover how things are similar (pairing tool) and that things can be piled up (piling tool). They also begin to get a sense of 'oneness', 'pairings' and 'lots' of objects. You can find out more about the learning tools in Chapter 4 (pp. 27–28).

Promoting the placing tool

It is a good idea to experiment with making some of the familiar material more exciting and at the same time extending the children's placing activity. Here is an idea for you to try and see whether the children copy you or not.

The placing game (for one child)

Skills

● Learning one-to-one correspondence

● Learning to sequence a series of actions.

Materials you will need

● A set of six to twelve clear jars with easy-to-screw-on lids.

● A set of the same number of similar objects. These could be, for example, 'toy men' without moveable limbs, large buttons, shells or keys.

● A small flat dish or an ice-cube tray with the same number of sections as jars and objects. (If you use a segmented tray like an ice-cube tray, then make sure that the objects are small enough to fit in.)

● Another container such as a small fruit basket.

Activity

● Either set this activity up at a small table or put out a large mat or small carpet or rug on the floor to create a 'contained' area.

- Put each of the objects into the jars and stand them together. Place the dish or segmented tray nearby.

- Demonstrate by unscrewing a jar, retrieving the object inside and then placing the object in the open tray (or if you have opted for the segmented tray, in one of the segments) and the lid in the basket.

- Allow the children to join in the play and let them carry on independently once they have got the idea themselves.

- When all the objects are in the tray, the activity can be reversed so that each of the objects is put back in the jars with the lids screwed back on.

This game can be played using zip-up purses or little boxes with lids instead of the jars, and you can vary the selection of objects as much as you like. If there are two or three children in the group, it is important that each child has their own set of materials. However, it works better with one child at a time, and there should never be more than three children.

Using tongs, spoons or sticks

Another way to make placing activities more interesting is to introduce a hand-held tool with which to pick up the objects, such as a spoon or tongs. Another idea is to use a stick to lift off or put on rings (such as bracelets or curtain rings) on a rod (kitchen-paper holder).

Promoting the banging tool

Making music

Toddlers and young children love to make music by shaking and banging objects that make sounds. There are plenty of musical instruments which can be purchased, but being imaginative about making shakers or finding things for children to make a banging noise is great fun.

Banging drums or xylophones to the count of a beat gives children their first experience of sequence and counting.

Take the children on a musical march as they march around the room or your garden to the beat of '1, 2, 3, 4!' You may feel a little like the Pied Piper, but the children will love this as they bang their drums.

Some ideas of objects for banging

- wooden spoons
- short dowel rods
- biscuit tins with lids
- small saucepans
- metal cake tins
- metal spoons
- chopsticks
- wooden boxes.

Nursery rhyme
Ten Little Fingers

I have ten little fingers,
And they all belong to me.
I can make them do things,
Would you like to see?
I can shut them tight,
Or open them all wide.
Put them together
Or make them all hide.
I can make them jump up high;
I can make them jump low.
I can fold them quietly,
And hold them just so.

Effective practice

- When playing games with young children, such as the Placing Game, choose a time when the children are alert and interested. Friday afternoon is probably not a good time!

- Children love to do things with adults, but sometimes they can get bored if activities are too difficult or if too many children are involved at the same time. It is a good idea to play with one child at a time until they show you that they are happy to play in a group of two.

- It is important to be flexible when playing games so that they can be adapted to the abilities and interests of the children.

Planning and resourcing

- Make sure that your role-play area is well stocked with sets of kitchen utensils, crockery, bedroom items and dressing-up clothes.

- When organising for a music session, make sure the children will not be interrupted (such as to go home) so that it can be a joyful shared experience.

Home links

- Share with parents the things you have noticed about their child's interest in numbers as key person Sally did in the example above.

- Take photos to share with the parents of the children at play.

- Invite parents to come in and observe a 'music session'.

- Ask parents to bring in objects for banging to add to your collection.

Additional resources

Umansky, K. (2000) *Three Tapping Teddies: Musical Stories and Chants for the Very Young,* London: A. & C. Black.

Also in the series are *Three Singing Pigs* and *Three Rapping Rats.*

From 30–50 months

Development matters

- Use some number names and number language spontaneously.
- Show curiosity about numbers by offering comments or asking questions.
- Use some number names accurately in play.
- Sometimes match number and quantity correctly.
- Recognise groups with one, two or three objects.

Key words

curiosity about numbers, using number names

What children have said or done

Here is an example of a four-year-old girl using number names and number language spontaneously.

> At the end of a long walk, Sarah was tired and wanted to get back to the nursery. I gave her reassuring comments but she reckoned that the remaining distance back to the nursery would be 'more than three steps and less than a billion'! I think this was her way of telling me that she had very little confidence that we would be there soon.

Children's first 'sense' of a number often comes from their age, and, with it, they feel an 'ownership' of that number. Here are a couple of examples, which I am sure you are familiar with.

- At register time, we count the children: one, two, three, four, etc. Sometimes as we go round, one of the children will object to the number they are given (for example, two) saying 'No! I'm not two, I'm three!' In this case, the children attach the number name they are hearing to themselves as a personal feature and do not yet understand the ordinal feature of the number as being a position in a list, in this case, second.

- Another time, a four-year-old boy heard that another boy was also identified as four. He strongly objected to this saying, 'But he can't be four! I'm four!' What may have happened here is that the little boy has probably heard several adults tell him he is four (referring to his age) and so he 'identifies' with it and cannot possibly imagine how anyone can share his identity. (This is what psychologists describe as being egocentric.)

Look, listen and note

- Enjoy the children's emerging interest in numbers and how they relate to their own personal lives and experiences.

- Children's first experience of number as having meaning for them is often their age, although there are misunderstandings as can be seen in the examples above.

Activities, objects and rhymes

Counting

Children of this age love to use counting words, because there is a sing-song quality to reciting them and they always get a good reaction from the grown-ups! However, at first they do not yet understand that numbers always go in the same order and see no reason why four should come after three so it does not matter if they say them in the wrong order. What is important is that what they say is accepted and enjoyed by you and that they hear the adults saying them in the right order.

Remember too that children of this age may be able to recite a counting sequence but most of them will not be ready to use the sequence to count a group of objects till they are at least four years old.

Practising counting during 'routines of the day'

There are plenty of opportunities for the children to be a part of counting during the routine of a day, whether you are working in a pre-school, nursery school, day-care nursery or your own home. Here are some examples:

- register time;

- setting the table;

- putting out cups and plates for snack time;

- counting out biscuits, pieces of fruit, raisins, etc., for each child in a group.

Simple number walk

When you take children for a walk round the setting, round the garden or outside, such as to the local shops or park, point out and talk together about the numbers of things you can see. Maybe there are three ducks on the pond, two lorries queuing at the traffic lights, three buggies out-side the door. The children will then begin to notice and tell you these things for themselves.

Number rhymes and fairy stories

I have already described the importance of singing nursery rhymes in Chapter 2 (p. 19). However, whereas the pleasure of rhymes for babies and toddlers comes from the intimacy of being cradled by their key person, for this age group the pleasure can be shared in a group. The fun of singing rhymes or chanting the key parts of a fairy story in a group led by the practitioner is very potent in helping children secure number or size sequences. Some commonly loved rhymes include:

- Ten Green Bottles

- Ten Little Monkeys Jumping on the Bed

- Ten in the Bed

- Five Little Ducks

- Five Little Speckled Frogs.

It is good to collect props such as a set of green bottles, monkey puppets, etc. so that not only the singing is brought to life but also the children begin to associate the sounds and words with real objects that they can see and handle for themselves. (It is possible to purchase 'ready-made' number rhymes with a bag of props, as suggested in the additional resources section on p. 64.)

Some commonly loved fairy stories include:

● The Three Little Pigs

● Goldilocks and the Three Bears

● Snow White and the Seven Dwarfs

● The Three Billy-Goats Gruff

● The Wolf and the Seven Little Kids.

Storytelling using real props is far more exciting for children in a group than reading from a book, however wonderful the illustrations. Many practitioners feel nervous about telling stories, because they feel foolish or wonder if their colleagues may laugh. Maybe you feel like that? Start with a story that you loved as a child and which is very familiar to you. Don't worry if it comes out 'wrong' (to you) because the children will love how you tell it anyway.

Extending nursery-rhyme and fairy-story themes

● Why not try making up your own stories or nursery rhymes about subjects which interest your children, using the tunes of traditional rhymes or the framework of familiar fairy stories.

● Create a lotto game based on the subject of a favourite nursery rhyme, such as ducks or frogs.

● Use beanbag frogs or small teddies, for example for counting games.

● Create a display area on the theme of a fairy story or nursery rhyme.

● Change your role-play area (or create a second role-play area) on the theme of something such as the cottage in 'Goldilocks and the Three Bears' to include different sizes of beds, tables, etc., as well as three of everything.

It is important to include the children in creating displays or new role-play areas as:

● it promotes confidence and initiative;

● it gives children opportunities to practise talking about numbers in meaningful ways.

Children are more likely to play with what they have created. However, what you may also find is that once something has been created they lose interest! It is often the creating which is interesting, but once it has been made they want to move on to something else.

● Take photos of the children involved in all these activities and make a simple number book.

● Make things such as frog masks or painted and laminated cardboard bottles with the children so they use them when acting out the rhyme.

The piggy-bank game

This game can be played with a group of two to four children right up to the age of sixty months and older.

Skills

● practising the counting sequence;

● using the counting sequence to determine quantity;

● learning invariance of number;

● experiencing permanence of objects removed from view.

Materials you will need

● An open box or tube with a wide slit cut into the bottom. (The end with the slit now becomes the top.)

● A handful of 'flat' objects that will fit through the slit, such as buttons, counters or small lids.

Activity

- Drop whatever number of objects is appropriate for this particular group of children through the slit of the box or tube as the children count out loud. You may start with only two objects then increase in number as the children grow in competence.

- Ask the children to tell you how many objects they think there will be when you lift the box or tube.

- Lift the box or tube and count together.

- Repeat for as long as the children are interested.

The piggy-bank game comes from Baratta-Lorton (1998).

 Nursery rhyme

There Were Ten in the Bed

There were ten in the bed and the little one said,
'Roll over! Roll over!'
So they all rolled over and one fell out.
Then there were nine in the bed and the little one said,
'Roll over! Roll over!'
So they all rolled over and one fell out.
Then there were eight in the bed and the little one said,
'Roll over! Roll over!'
[And so on, until …]
Then there was one in the bed and the little one said,
'Goodnight!'

Effective practice

- It is important to recognise the important opportunities for children to learn and experience counting through participating in the routines of the day. Allow children to help you, where possible.

- When setting up 'number' activities and games, make sure that there is a maximum of four children, otherwise they will lose interest.

- Stories and nursery rhymes are a wonderfully social way of promoting the learning of number skills especially with a small group of children and the use of 'props'.

Planning and resourcing

- Take advantage of the opportunities for counting and experiencing numbers through visits or walks outside the setting as well as providing number labels and number games in your outdoor play area.

- Use your public library for further books of stories and rhymes as well as music CDs.

Home links

- Share your 'stories' of the children's use of number words with parents and encourage them to do the same.

- Take photos of the children playing number games and taking part in music, rhymes and stories to show the parents how their children are having fun with numbers.

- Be sure to let parents know that the children are 'playing with number words' and whilst they are enjoying the counting sequence, they do not necessarily understand how to use this sequence to count a group of objects.

Parents need to be reassured that children's understanding of number comes from playing and experiencing numbers in their everyday lives. They are not old enough to be doing any kind of 'sums'. Indeed, even counting more than three objects reliably does not usually happen before a child is four years old.

Additional resources

(♪)   Number rhyme bags from Early Excellence, www.earlyexcellence. com.

(📖)   Baratta-Lorton, M. (ed.) (1998) *Mathematics Their Way: An Activity-Centred Mathematics Programme for Early Childhood,* Boston, Mass.: Addison Wesley Longman.

(♪)   MacGregor, H. (1998) *Tom Thumb's Musical Maths,* London: A&C Black.

From 40–60 months

Development matters

- Recognise some numerals of personal significance.

- Count up to three or four objects by saying one number name for each item.

- Count out up to six objects from a larger group.

- Count actions or objects that cannot be moved.

- Begin to count beyond ten.

- Begin to represent numbers using fingers, marks on paper or pictures.

- Select the correct numeral to represent one to five, then one to nine objects.

- Recognise numerals 1 to 5.

- Count an irregular arrangement of up to ten objects.

- Estimate how many objects they can see and check by counting them.

- Count aloud in ones, twos, fives and tens.

- Know that numbers identify how many objects are in a set.

- Use ordinal numbers in different contexts.

- Match then compare the number of objects in two sets.

Early learning goals

- Say and use number names in order in familiar contexts.
- Count reliably up to ten everyday objects.
- Recognise numerals 1 to 9.
- Use mathematical ideas and methods to solve practical problems.

Key words

recognising numerals, knowing numbers identify how many, counting beyond ten

What children have said or done

Here is an example of a five-year-old girl, Jenny thinking about numbers of personal significance following a visit to her Great Granny.

> Great Granny is very old. She's eighty-six. Her friend Sophie Johnson is not quite as old. She's seventy-five. Granny's much younger because she's her daughter. She's sixty. Mummy is only thirty-five and has got some grey hair.

Children of this age are fascinated by age, and this little girl has got a sophisticated grasp of number ages. However, a younger girl in a pre-school guessed her key person was thirteen years old. (She was in fact forty!) In this case, the little girl thought her key person was much older than her (quite rightly) and chose one of the biggest numbers she could think of.

Look, listen and note

Notice the numbers children are interested in as they will relate to their own lives, such as family ages, house numbers, etc. At this age, children begin to take a great interest in written numerals. Share in this interest and extend it by pointing out numbers in their experience, such as those on a telephone, bus, recipe, etc.

Activities, objects and rhymes

It is important to create what is often described as a number-rich environment for children of pre-school age so they have the opportunity to see and use written numerals in many different contexts. Here are some simple ideas that you might like to try in your setting. Maybe you have tried them already but have not done them in a while? Maybe these ideas reflect what you already have. If that is the case, then take heart, you are providing a number rich environment!

- **Number signs**. Put up numbers on things such as the toilet doors, the children's pegs (as well as pictures), etc. You might like to put numbers on the toy bikes or other wheeled toys and chalk numbered parking spaces (for outside only).

- **Number lines**. There are lots of ways of creating number lines, and you can be as creative as you like. The most important thing is to create them with the children and to display them at the children's level. Here are some number-line ideas:

  - *Objects number line.* Laminate eleven A4 pieces of card each with a clear number from 0 to 10 displayed at the bottom. Then lay these cards out in a line and put the right number of objects on each card, leaving the one with '0' empty.

  - *Photos number line.* Do the same as for the objects but this time take photos of objects and stick them on with Blu Tack so they can be removed and new pictures used from time to time.

  - *Photos of the children number line.* Take photos of individual children and put the right number of children's pictures against each numeral on the line. Alternatively, take a photo of one child, then another photo with two children, then another with three and so on until you have ten children standing in a line together.

  - *Ten bottles number line.* Collect ten wide necked clear plastic bottles, filling each with a different number of corks and closing them securely. Label each bottle clearly with the number on the outside. Put string around the neck of each bottle and hang them from hooks on a line on the wall. Alternatively you can simply stand the bottles in a line and have no need for string.

- **Number hunt**. Children love treasure hunts and they can find fun in hunting for anything! You could 'hide' numbers on cards (maybe four or five of each) around the room or garden. The children are each given a card with a number printed on it and then they have to hunt for as many cards as they can that match their number card.

- **Posting game.** This is a bit like the number-hunt game. However, this time you need to collect ten cardboard boxes. On one of the sides paint or draw a door and make a wide slit for posting. Put these 'doors' around the room or garden. The children are then given a collection of envelopes (which they can pretend are letters) with numbers on them. They have to post the letters in the right door.

- **Number walk**. You could take a group of children on a walk and look for how many things in their environment have numbers on them. These may include road signs, car number plates, numbers on buses, house numbers and so on.

- **Noticing numbers.** When children begin to notice and talk about numbers with you (spontaneously), respond with interest and appreciation even if what they tell you is not strictly accurate. You may like to write down what the children say and keep their comments as a record of their understanding of number and notice their progress over time. Children learn about numbers through their own interests, observation and activity. They do not need to be taught numbers.

- **Writing numbers.** When children are ready, they will want to try writing numbers. At first, numbers are often formed back to front. This is quite normal. Allow children the opportunity to 'write' numbers with their fingers only in sand, cornflour, on your back or in the palm of your hand. Children may also want to paint, draw or chalk numbers on paper or the hard ground outside (paving stones, concrete, etc.).

Spill the beans game

This game can be played with children (for a group of no more than three to four children) right up to the age of sixty months and older.

Skills

● Practising the counting sequence.

● Using the counting sequence to determine quantity.

● Learning invariance of number.

Materials you will need

● A small drawstring bag.

● Dried beans (or other objects, which are easy to pick up and hold such as pebbles, small wooden bricks or drinks bottle tops).

● A bell.

Activity

● Counting aloud, place as many beans as appropriate (no more than three to begin with). The children then pass the bag around the group until they hear you ring the bell, which is the signal for everyone to call out, 'Spill the beans!'

● Ask the children to predict how many beans there will be when counted.

● The child with the bag empties it out, and everyone then counts the beans together (to reinforce the concept of invariance).

● The beans are then put back in the bag, and the game continues until the children lose interest. (As children become more competent, then only the child who has the bag does the actual counting.)

Alix, an early years practitioner in a pre-school gives an account of when she played this game with a small group of four-year-olds.

I explained and demonstrated the game, then we all had a go. Instead of beans, I used plastic building blocks. The children quickly grasped the rules and could all correctly guess the number when the bell rang. I extended the game by letting the children put the blocks in the bag. They liked this and soon had their own ideas! First they wanted to take charge of ringing the bell then they wanted to each have a turn at putting the blocks in as they passed the bag round. The first child counted as he put in three blocks. The next child put in four blocks counting on from four to seven. The third child put in two blocks and they all counted to nine. The fourth child rang the bell. As the game went on, they often waited two rounds before ringing the bell and the highest number they counted to altogether was fourteen. One child even got to nineteen on his turn! (He is particularly interested in numbers.) The children extended the game further by hiding the fourteen blocks around them and ringing the bell to start finding them! The children really enjoyed the game, spending twenty minutes on it. When we have played it again, they always start with the original version of the game.

This account illustrates not only how children of four years of age can play cooperatively but also how playing in a group allows them to develop their number and problem-solving skills and to use their imaginations. Alix, as the guiding adult, has given the children the framework by showing them the game but has also allowed them the freedom to develop their own ideas. This demonstrates how the early years practitioner is a facilitator in children's learning.

The spill the beans game comes from Baratta-Lorton (1998).

 ## Nursery rhyme

One, Two, Buckle My Shoe

One, two, buckle my shoe,
Three, four, knock at the door,
Five, six, pick up sticks,
Seven, eight, lay them straight,
Nine, ten a big fat hen,

Eleven, twelve, dig and delve,
Thirteen, fourteen, maids a-courting,
Fifteen, sixteen, maids in the kitchen,
Seventeen, eighteen, maids in waiting,
Nineteen, twenty, my plate's empty!

Effective practice

It is important that the children observe the adults using numbers in their daily routines as they learn about the purpose of counting in this way.

Make sure that there are no more than four children playing a structured game with 'turns'; otherwise, they will become bored, and it will spoil both their pleasure and the learning opportunity.

When playing games, you may find that the more able children want to adapt or extend them. Whenever you see this happen, allow it to develop naturally but give a helping hand if they are finding it difficult to cooperate with each other.

Planning and resourcing

- Create a 'number-rich' environment both indoors and outdoors.

- Make sure there are opportunities for children to draw or write numbers through providing chalks, crayons, pencils and paints. It is also great to 'finger draw' numbers in sand, 'gloop' (cornflour and water), mud, etc.

- When playing structured number games, allow enough time so the children can continue for as long as they are interested.

Home links

Parents often 'worry' that their children should be doing sums or be taught how to write numbers. It is important that parents are reassured that children of this age need to 'experience' and to 'play' with numbers in order to learn about them. It is damaging to children to introduce them to formal learning of mathematics too early.

Additional resources

Baratta-Lorton, M. (ed.) (1998) *Mathematics Their Way: An Activity-Centred Mathematics Programme for Early Childhood,* Boston, Mass.: Addison Wesley Longman.

Beswick, C. (2005) *The Little Book of Colour, Shape and Number,* Lutterworth: Featherstone Education Ltd.

Clere, L. (2004) *The Little Book of Bags Boxes & Trays,* Lutterworth: Featherstone Education Ltd.

Lewisham Early Years Advice and Resource Network (2002) *A Place to Learn: Developing a Stimulating Environment,* Lewisham: Lewisham Early Years Advice and Resource Network.

Skinner, C. (2002) *More than Numbers: Children Developing Mathematical Thinking.* Early Education.

For further ideas, please refer to the Additional Resources section at the end of 'From 40–60 months' in Chapter 7 (p. 101).

The EYFS principles

The four principles which guide the work of all early years practitioners are discussed on pp. 31–33. Please refer to this for a greater understanding of how to put the principles into practice.

7 Calculating

From birth–20 months

Development matters

- Are logical thinkers from birth.
- Have some understanding that things exist, even when out of sight.
- Are alert to and investigate things that challenge their expectations.

Key words

objects exist, investigation

What children have said or done

This is an observation of Sam, who is sixteen months old and is playing with a collection of different-sized tins and a soft toy penguin.

> Sam is happy playing with his heuristic-play materials, and today he has got his soft toy penguin with him. The penguin is about 30 centimetres tall. Sam starts to pile the tins one on top of the other, but they go up in a random order and one disappears inside another as the tower grows. Sam does not seem to notice. As the tower gets taller, Sam stands up to be able to reach to the top.

Eventually he takes a pause, looks at the tower and gets excited by it. He knocks it down, and the tins scatter around him. Sam then sees his penguin and picks it up and tries putting it in one of the tins. The penguin is far too large and simply balances on top. Sam then tries putting the penguin in a larger tin. Still the penguin will not fit. Sam then sees the largest tin and picks up his penguin and tries again. The penguin slides inside easily and almost disappears from view. Sam shows his delight by standing with rigid limbs and making excited squealing-type sounds. Within moments Sam notices some lids and goes over to play with them.

In the observation, Sam demonstrated placing and piling learning tools and the experience of 'small and large'.

Look, listen and note

- When children of this age are playing with open-ended materials (heuristic play), it is important to give yourself the time to sit comfortably and watch what they are doing.

- In a short space of time a toddler can carry out several different 'experiments' and learn several concepts, which could be easily missed. It is important to notice what toddlers are doing because you will get an idea of their particular interests and of how their play is becoming increasingly sophisticated.

- Toddlers need to know you are 'there' in order to feel safe and secure and to know they can share their pleasure with you.

Activities, objects and rhymes

Treasure basket

The most stimulating play material to offer babies is a treasure basket (see Chapter 6, pp. 37–42, where I describe the best way to offer the treasure basket and suggest 100 or so objects you can collect). It really is the most magical of all play material for a seated baby who is not yet crawling because it provides the opportunity for:

- choice;

- extended periods of concentration;

- investigation of a variety of objects;

- independent thinking.

Another activity that involves objects is 'Hide the object!' Choose a favourite object and give it to the baby. When the baby offers it to you, take it and hide it under a piece of cloth (such as a scarf). See if the baby knows where it has gone! If not, pick up the piece of cloth and have a bit of fun together discovering it is still there. This is a bit like the peek-a-boo game. It is a baby's first experience of absence and presence, which is also about the numbers 0 and 1.

Heuristic play

When a baby begins to crawl and wants to move objects from place to place (the placing tool) then the treasure basket no longer holds the same kind of interest. If toddlers had language, they would be asking 'What can I do with this object?' Toddlers want to investigate how objects respond if they are thrown, posted, rolled, piled up and so on. For this reason, it is really important to have plenty of containers in which objects can be placed. It is also important to have collections of several different sets of objects.

This type of play is called heuristic play and has been described in more detail in Chapters 4 and 6 (pp. 28–30, 45–48). See Chapter 6 for the best way to offer this material and a suggested list of containers and objects.

 ## Nursery rhyme

One Potato, Two Potato

One potato, two potato,
Three potato, four,
Five potato, six potato,
Seven potato, more!

Toddler at heuristic play

Effective practice

The practitioner needs to be attentive to how the children play alongside one another. One child might grab another child's object but is too young to understand what 'sharing' means. Make sure that both the children have objects to satisfy their interest.

Have fun when playing peek-a-boo games and be ready to respond to children at intimate times such as nappy changing or when you and a child have a cuddle together.

Planning and resourcing

- Make sure that there is enough material for a small group of children to play and explore in the confidence that there will be plenty to go round.

- When selecting objects for the children to play with, make sure that they are safe, clean and unbroken and discard anything that is no longer in good quality condition.

- Regularly add new objects to the treasure basket and make new collections for your heuristic play bags.

Home links

- It is important to explain to parents how the children are developing problem-solving skills when playing with open-ended materials in the treasure basket or during heuristic play sessions.

- Many parents need reassurance that everyday objects are safe and have sound educational value. Encourage them to come and join in a session or take photographs of the children when they are playing to show parents at the end of the day.

Additional resources

Goldschmied, E. and Hughes, A. M. (1992) *Heuristic Play with Objects* (film), London: National Children's Bureau. Reproduced in 2007 on DVD.

Goldschmied, E. and Jackson, S. (2003) *People Under Three: Young Children in Day Care*, 2nd edn, Oxford: Routledge.

Hughes, A. M. (2006) *Developing Play for the Under Threes: The Treasure Basket and Heuristic Play*, London: David Fulton.

Jenson, W. and Channon, J. (2004) *Echo Fred: Songs for the Very Young*, www.kidsmusiceducation.com.

From 16–36 months

Development matters

- Are learning to classify by organising and arranging toys with increasing intent.

- Categorise objects according to their properties.

- Begin to make comparisons between quantities.

- Know that a group of things changes in quantity when something is added or taken away.

Key words

classification, organisation, comparison

What children have said or done

This is an observation of a girl who came into the playroom after playing in the garden of her nursery setting.

> She came inside clutching five stones, which she had found on the shingle path. She took them to one of the tables and carefully placed them one after the other in a line on the table. She picked them up and repeated this again. Then she fetched a small raffia basket with a handle and dropped the stones in one after the other. This did not feel right to her, so she got another basket, this time a much larger one, and carefully put the stones in one by one. They loosely fitted inside the basket but still she was not satisfied! She searched and found a third basket. The size of this basket was in between the other two. Once again she carefully dropped the five stones inside, one by one. A smile came over her face and she held it up with great satisfaction.

This is a marvellous illustration of how children are able to set their own problems and make calculations to work out the solutions without any

Sorting stones I

direct involvement from an adult. This little girl needed no encouragement because she was confident that the atmosphere was calm and the adults were nearby (see photographs on pp. 78–82).

Look, listen and note

- When children feel safe and secure in their relationships with their key persons, they are able to play independently and with confidence.

- Take time to observe what the children are doing in their play as their problem-solving ideas can be surprising and fascinating, which the example above illustrates.

- It is easy to miss the detail of what individual children are doing in the hustle and bustle of general activity. Notice those who seem engrossed and busy and see how long they actually play at a task they have set themselves.

Sorting stones II

Activities, objects and rhymes

At this age, children are developing three of their learning tools, namely: pairing, matching and sorting. These learning tools are vital mental tools for children in developing their calculating skills. You can read more about the learning tools in Chapter 4. Below are some ideas you might like to try with individual children or a small group of no more than three.

When setting up materials for activities it is worth taking note of the following points:

- The way you set out an activity may vary according to a child's age, so it is important to 'experiment' and see how enthusiastic a child is. (This is the best guide as to whether you have gauged the level correctly or not.)

- It is useful to take the children's 'lead' and then support them, rather than the other way round.

- Beware! It is easy to take the lead yourself when you set up material as an 'activity', but the children may either show no interest

Sorting stones III

or simply 'please you' till they create their 'own game'. Either way, it is not as exciting for the children nor is it satisfying for you as the practitioner.

Pairing baskets game

For a group of one to three children.

Skills

●   Practising the pairing tool.

●   Learning one-to-one correspondence.

Materials you will need

●   A small rigid basket (such as one for fruit).

●   Pairs of identical objects (ten to twenty pairs). The objects could include a pair of socks, spoons, CDs, dolly pegs, same-coloured hair rollers, scouring sponges, wooden doorknobs, 50-pence coins,

Sorting stones IV

bracelets, identical pairs of animals, identical pairs of toy vehicles, coasters, napkin rings, lolly sticks, champagne corks. The possibilities are endless, but it is important to find identical pairs of objects rather than simply those that are similar.

• Two further containers, such as the plastic trays for large plant pots or containers for fruit from the supermarket.

Activity

• Either set up this activity at a low table or put out a large mat, small carpet or rug on the floor to create a 'contained' area.

• Put all the pairs of objects into the large basket with the empty two containers on either side.

• Demonstrate what to do by picking out a pair of objects and putting one in one tray and the other in the other tray.

• Allow the children to join in the play and carry on independently once they have got the idea and are happy for you to be there, simply to watch and be a supportive presence.

Sorting stones V

- You can talk about the objects, naming them and saying what they are used for.

- When all the objects have been separated into the two trays then they can be tipped back in the basket and the game can start again.

Extending the pairing basket game: find the pair!

- You may like to select a few objects from around the room and put them in a large pocket (of a tabard apron) or in a drawstring bag.

- Pull out one of the objects and show it to the children and invite them to find its pair.

- When they bring the object, check with them that it is exactly the same and put these 'same' objects in a large container such as a tin.

- Continue until the children show no more interest or until you have run out of objects in your pocket or bag.

Beans in a cup

For one to three children from age thirty months upwards only.

Skills

- Learning about comparisons.

- Beginning to get a sense of the number two.

Materials you will need

- A handful of large beans such as dried kidney beans, placed in a dish or bowl. (It is important to supervise the children carefully in this activity to ensure that they do not put the beans in their mouths as they are poisonous when eaten. However, they are perfectly safe for handling.)

- Several paper fairy-cake holders or foil mince-pie dishes.

Activity

- Place the bowl of beans at a table where children will not be knocked into by other children.

- Put out some of the paper holders.

- Put one bean in one of the holders, saying 'This is one bean' aloud as you do so.

- Invite the children to do the same.

- Put two beans in a holder counting aloud as you do so.

- Invite the children to do the same.

- See if the children carry on putting in one or two beans, using a pointing finger to count how many are in the holder. It does not matter if they get it wrong.

- You may want to empty the beans from the holders back in the bowl so the game can continue, once you have used up all the paper cake holders.

Exploring volume

It is important to include ladles, spoons and cups as well as different sizes of jars in trays of water, sand, dried rice, dried lentils, etc.

In this way, children can experiment with different quantities and how they look different in different shaped containers. It is through the experience of playing around with this kind of material that children begin to get the idea of conservation of volume. This is when children realise that two amounts can be the same even though one may look greater depending on the shape of the container.

It is important to provide a range of transparent containers. Under supervision, glass jars are perfectly safe, although it is preferable to play where the ground beneath the sand, water or builder's tray is not too hard. The usual hard floor surfaces in a playroom are fine. However, ceramic-tile floors or concrete or tarmac may not be suitable when children are playing with glass jars.

Some ideas for transparent jars

- jam or marmalade jars
- pesto jars
- pickle jars
- baby food jars
- instant-coffee jars
- mustard jars.

A small tip!

Soak any jars in a bowl of cold water till the labels peel off (or are loose enough for you to peel off). In this way the children can see clearly how much sand, water, etc., is in the jars.

Nursery rhyme

Indians

One little, two little, three little Indians,
Four little, five little, six little Indians,
Seven little, eight little, nine little Indians,
Ten little Indian boys.

Effective practice

- When playing structured 'number games' such as pairing baskets or beans in a cup, try them out first of all with one child only. In this way, you get a 'feel' as to how the game will work in your setting.

- It is important to choose times when children are 'in the mood' for adult-led activity to play structured games. They are unlikely to want to play a structured game when they are in the middle of their self-chosen play or when they are tired, hungry or in distress.

Planning and resourcing

- It is a good idea to buy and collect several different-sized transparent containers as well as spoons and ladles, so the children have plenty of opportunity to fill and empty and experiment with seeing the volume of water, dry sand, rice, etc., in a small group. (If you are unhappy with using glass, then there are plenty of plastic jars available from which to choose.)

- If you have the space, the jars could be stored on a shelf marked with coloured silhouettes to further help the children with matching size and shape when tidying up.

Home links

- Explain to parents why you are using materials such as glass and dried kidney beans as they may be concerned about the safety of their children.

- Reassure parents that their children will be supervised and that it is important for them to take safe risks by handling material such as thick glass jars carefully. It is only when children use fragile material and material from their everyday world that they are able to learn how to take care and think about what they are doing.

- Encourage parents to involve their children in simple tasks around the home such as filling or emptying the washing machine, putting pairs of socks together for folding, sorting out underwear into 'Mummy's', 'Daddy's' and 'mine'.

- Take photos of the children when they are playing with sand, water, dried rice, etc., and share your pleasure with parents about how their children are learning from this type of play.

Additional resources

Thomas, S. (2002) *Familiar Things: Can Do Play Activity Series,* London: Thomson Learning.

Tumble Tots Action Songs, Avid Records, www.avidgroup.co.uk.

From 30–50 months

Development matters

- Compare two groups of objects, saying when they have the same number.

- Show an interest in number problems.

- Separate a group of three or four objects in different ways, beginning to recognise that the total is still the same.

Key words

same and different

What children have said or done

Tom is four years old and has been attending a nursery since he was a toddler. He knows the children in his room very well. This is what his key person wrote about his interest in numbers:

> I have noticed that Tom is interested in how many children are *not* in nursery, rather than counting how many are present. It seems he has a perception of a 'set' as a normal 'whole' and when there is a lesser quantity he sees this as an abnormality that requires explanation.

 ## Look, listen and note

Children as young as four years are actively noticing 'amounts' of things, including numbers of people in their lives. They are developing a clear sense of quantity as is illustrated in the extract above describing Tom's interest in the presence or absence of children in his nursery.

Activities, objects and rhymes

Matching and sorting

At this age, children spend a lot of time preoccupied with matching and sorting objects in various different ways. They are practising the learning tools of matching and sorting. You can find out more about these learning tools in Chapter 4.

Unlike pairing, where children put together pairs of identical items, matching involves putting together pairs or groups of similar as well as identical items. Indeed, matching develops the skills of comparing and contrasting. Whilst children are getting a sense of the characteristics of different objects, such as matching for colour, function or maybe a sensory feature such as roughness, they are also experiencing the characteristic of quantity. They begin to calculate whether there are 'one' or 'lots' of things and whether there are 'more' or 'less' even though they may not yet be able to reliably count out more than two objects accurately.

Once children have got the idea of matching, this naturally leads to sorting, and it is important to create collections of objects for the children to be able to do sorting tasks. You can buy commercially produced material for sorting, but this tends to be expensive, made out of plastic and has no relationship with the child's real world. It is much more fun and interesting to create your own collections of objects for sorting.

Some ideas of objects for sorting

- keys (individual not in bunches)
- pegs
- shells
- curtain rings
- egg cups (metal or wood)
- marbles
- lids
- coasters

Keys

- bricks (preferably wooden)
- small bean bags
- ribbons
- spoons
- small brushes
- toy cars
- wicker balls
- cotton reels
- toy animals (farm, zoo and pet).

There are further ideas of objects for sorting in Chapter 8 in the section for 30–50 months (see pp. 125–126).

Find me some others!

For one to no more than four children.

Shells

Skills

- Learning about matching by name.

- Learning how to sort.

Materials you will need

- A small square of carpet for each child taking part in the activity.

- An 'example object' for each child.

Activity

- Put out the carpet squares in a safe corner of the room where they will not be walked on.

- Give each child an object, such as a brick, toy car, toy horse, etc.

- Show them the carpet squares and allocate one to each child.

- Invite the children to put the object on the carpet square and look around the playroom for as many different versions of their object as they can.

This game can be as simple or as elaborate as you and the children want to make it and can develop into searching for objects with different criteria rather than by 'name'. It could be they might want to look for objects that are 'shiny' (feature), 'round' (shape), 'bathroom' (theme), 'wooden' (material), 'old' (quality) and so on.

You might want to give each child a bucket in which to collect their objects rather than using a carpet square.

Matching, sorting and counting in everyday life

There are plenty of opportunities for children to engage in matching, sorting and counting in their everyday lives at your setting. Children of this age love to help the adults in real tasks. First of all you need to identify the routines of the day which require some organisation, and that will give you some ideas. However, in order to help you with this, here are some typical tasks that children are regularly involved with.

- Setting the table with cups, plates, knives and forks. (It is good to use 'silhouette' placemats to help children find the right positions for placing things such as the knives and forks. You can make these mats yourself and laminate them or cover them in clear sticky-backed plastic.)

- Sharing out items with a group of children. This may include putting out a set of plates and putting two pieces of fruit, biscuits, sandwiches, etc., on each plate.

- 'Tidying up' is a typical time when children are sorting, matching and counting and gives the children the satisfaction of creating order in their environment.

- Helping to create a display area or role-play area for the particular theme you are working on. Themes might include a new baby, fruits and vegetables, the seaside, insects and bugs and so on.

- Setting out outdoor play material (such as bikes, bats and balls). Children love to be part of setting up a play area, and this helps them become more responsible with the care of the equipment and material.

Nursery rhyme

Five Little Monkeys

Five little monkeys jumping on the bed,
One fell off and bumped his head.
Mama called the Doctor and the Doctor said,
'No more monkeys jumping on the bed!'

Four little monkeys jumping on the bed,
One fell off and bumped her head.
Papa called the Doctor and the Doctor said,
'No more monkeys jumping on the bed!'

Three little monkeys jumping on the bed,
One fell off and bumped his head,
Mama called the Doctor and the Doctor said,
'No more monkeys jumping on the bed!'

Two little monkeys jumping on the bed,
One fell off and bumped her head,
Papa called the Doctor and the Doctor said,
'No more monkeys jumping on the bed!'

One little monkey jumping on the bed,
He fell off and bumped his head,
Mama called the Doctor and the Doctor said,
'Put those monkeys straight to bed!'

Effective practice

- When you play structured games with young children, it is best to play with no more than two at a time until they are about forty-two months, when you can try playing with three children. It is not until children reach about four years old that they can enjoy playing in a group as large as four children.

- Invite children to help you in the everyday routines, wherever possible. Not only do children love to be helpful at this age, they will also be learning about feeling trusted and responsible. They will learn the practical skills such as pouring and sweeping and the mental skills of counting, matching, sorting and calculating.

Planning and resourcing

- Make sure that your role-play area is well equipped with collections and sets of materials such as cutlery, pegs, plates, cups, pairs of shoes or socks, small boxes or packets, toy fruit, etc., so your children experience matching, pairing and comparing amounts of objects.

- Telling stories and singing nursery rhymes are very good ways of giving children the chance to enjoy becoming familiar with numbers. Include props such as pictures or real objects to make it really come alive for the children.

Home links

- Tell the parents about how the children like to do sorting and show them your sorting materials so they can appreciate the value of using everyday materials.

- Encourage the parents to collect objects for sorting by putting up lists of objects on your notice board and asking them to make collections to bring in. The larger the collections, the better!

Additional resources

- Website for nursery rhymes related to counting: www.songsforteaching.com/numberscounting.htm.

From 40–60 months

Development matters

- Find the total number of items in two groups by counting all of them.
- Use own methods to work through a problem.
- Say the number that is one more than a given number.
- Select two groups of objects to make a given total of objects.
- Count repeated groups of the same size.
- Share objects into equal groups and count how many in each group.

Early learning goals

- In practical activities and discussion, begin to use the vocabulary involved in adding and subtracting.
- Use language such as 'more' or 'less' to compare two numbers.
- Find one more or one less than a number from one to ten.
- Begin to relate addition to combining two groups of objects and subtraction to 'taking away'.

Key words

counting, sharing out, making comparisons

What children have said or done

This is what a secondary-school teacher told me recently about her daughter, Emily, who is fifty-three months old.

> Emily likes to watch me when I am marking the homework of my pupils. She is very curious about the marks that I give the children as she now recognises the numbers I write and understands a bit

about their value. She knows that the numbers 6 to 8 are good marks while those under 6 are not so good. I wish my pupils had such an acute perception of the value of my marks!

I also make piles of books on a shelf, in two sections: those which have been marked and those I still have to do. Emily keeps a countdown of how much work I still have left to do.

Look, listen and note

Children of this age can vary a great deal in their interest or competence in number. In the example above, Emily is clearly a very able and observant four-year-old. However, some children may still be at the stage of simply making comparisons between quantities without any detailed knowledge or understanding or number values.

It is important to listen to what the children are saying to you and to observe how they play with objects so that you are able to assess how much they understand. If children are 'forced' into number games and activities too early, before they are ready or interested, they will be 'put off' numbers. This could then have a negative effect on their learning.

Activities, objects and rhymes

Making comparisons

The skill of making comparisons develops from the learning tools of pairing, matching and sorting. It contributes an important step to a child's growing mathematical understanding. However, children begin to make comparisons using concrete familiar objects as numbers are too abstract for children of this age.

First of all, children like to make comparisons of equal groups of things. They like to focus on making them the same. This creates a standard that leads to children making future comparisons of more and less.

Sharing out

Children love to help adults, especially when it comes to food! There are plenty of opportunities you can create for children to participate in 'sharing out activities'.

- Allow a child to be 'in charge' of sharing out equal amounts of pieces of fruit, biscuits, sandwiches, raisins, etc. Start by suggesting the child puts two sandwiches, for example, on each plate.

- As children become more competent you might like to give them a packet of something, such as jelly baby sweets, and ask them to share them out equally into, let's say, six bowls.

- Opportunities like this allow you to help children gain an understanding of and to begin to use words such as 'enough', 'lots', 'more', 'less', 'many', etc.

Playing outside

There are many possibilities for solving problems and making comparisons outside. You just need to provide some basic materials and offer the children a few ideas.

- Suggest to children they could estimate how many pebbles or tree blocks might fit in different-sized containers such as a range of flower pots or small cardboard boxes. This could lead to discussion about why some will hold more or less, depending on the size of the containers and the size of the pebbles.

- Count how many bikes, cars, prams, hoops, planks, barrels, tyres, large bricks, large cones, pegs on a line, etc., there are and make comparisons of more, less and the same.

- Suggest to the children they might like to create a long bridge with planks, tyres and crates and see what happens. They will probably have many further ideas that you would have never thought of.

- The more the children play with open-ended everyday material, the more they are likely to come up with inventive ideas and problems to solve.

Suggested resources for playing outside

- tree-trunk sections

- tree blocks

- planks of wood (you can get these cut to order by a DIY store)

- sanded wooden offcuts

- bricks

- plastic crates (for bread or milk or from a supermarket)

- carpet squares

- plastic flower pots (of various shapes and sizes)

- large cones

- hoops and wooden embroidery rings

- cable spools

- large cardboard boxes

- plastic buckets of various sizes

- industrial tubing

- lengths of guttering

- lengths of drainpipe

- wooden blocks (assorted sizes, solid and hollow)

- lengths of rope

- hooks (positioned around the outdoor area ready for attaching rope, pulleys, pieces of sheet, etc.)

- plastic sheeting

- sheets, old bedspreads, table cloths, curtains, etc.

- lengths of hosepipe

- coloured chalks

- separate areas of pea shingle, sand, earth, pebbles (in large sand tray or contained within wooden frame)

- broom handles for attaching number signs, washing lines for numbers, etc.

- washing-up bowls containing collections of seasonal leaves, fruits, etc. (such as conkers, conker husks, leaves, snail shells, twigs, pieces of bark, etc.)

See Chapter 8 (pp. 137–139) for further resource ideas to play with outside.

Sorting by senses game

For a group of two to four children.

Skills

- Observing and describing properties of objects.

- Noticing similarities and differences.

- Connecting an abstract idea to the real world.

- Comparing.

- Using all the senses to gain information.

Materials you will need

- A collection of objects (borrowed from your treasure basket).

- Several jars of food, jams or spices.

Preparation

- Put small pieces of different foods on individual dishes, such as banana, marmite on toast, lemon, pickle, salted crisps, pizza, etc. Use your imagination! However, you will need to check if the children have any allergies to particular foods.

Activity

- Invite the children to taste the individual foods and describe whether they think they are sweet, sour, spicy or salty.

- The children can now take turns wearing a blindfold. Each of the other children can take turns handing an object to the one with the blindfold. The blindfolded child has to describe the object by texture, weight, size, shape and any other attributes they feel.

- Invite the children to try smelling the individual jars and then identifying the items by categories of their choice.

- The children could also focus on what different sounds are like by closing their eyes and telling if a noise is near or far, loud or soft.

- You may only wish to 'play around' with one sense at a time as the children may not sustain their interest in 'sorting by senses' for all of them at one session.

The sorting by senses game comes from Baratta-Lorton (1998).

 ## Nursery rhyme

Five Little Snowmen

Five little snowmen were very fat,
Each one wore a funny hat;
Out came the sun and melted one,
And four little snowmen stood in the sun.

(Continue counting down to one.)

One little snowman was very sad,
He still had his funny hat,
Down came the snow
And the children played,
And built four more snowmen on that winter's day!

Stephanie Burton, www.songsforteaching.com/
stephanieburton/5littlesnowmen.htm

Effective practice

- Give the children plenty of opportunity to be creative in their play, so they can develop their ideas together by offering open–ended materials such as the resources listed for playing outside.

- It is important to make sure that any structured games are short enough to sustain the children's interest.

- If children want to change the rules of a game you have set up, let them do so as planning and negotiating are important problem-solving skills.

Planning and resourcing

- When you set up a game such as the 'sorting by senses', make sure you have all the materials ready before you invite any of the children to join you.

- Invite parents to help you build up your resources for outdoor play, such as providing guttering, old sheets, etc.

 ## Home links

- Some parents might be concerned that you are using everyday or building materials in the outdoor area rather than bought toys. Explain how the children are able to be flexible and creative in their thinking and play and reassure them of the safety of the material.

- Take photos of the children playing a game with their key person to show to parents so they can see how you work with them in a group.

- Encourage parents to bring in 'old clothes' and wellingtons for their children to wear when playing outside, so they can freely get muddy or messy in any weather conditions.

- Explain to parents the value of playing outside (in all weathers) and be supportive and understanding to those parents who feel anxious about this. (Again, you might like to take photos to show parents how much their children enjoy the outside play.)

Additional resources

- Asco Educational Supplies Ltd, www.ascoeducational.co.uk

- Baratta-Lorton, M. (ed.) (1998) *Mathematics Their Way: An Activity-Centred Mathematics Programme for Early Childhood,* Boston, Mass.: Addison Wesley Longman. For more information, www.center.edu.

- Bayley, R. and Broadbent, L. (2001) *50 Exciting Things to Do Outside,* Lawrence Educational Publications.

- Bilton, H. (2004) *Playing Outside: Activities, Ideas and Inspiration for the Early Years,* London: David Fulton.

- Featherstone, S. (2001) *The Little Book of Outdoor Play,* Leicester: Featherstone Education Ltd.

- Pound, L. (1999) *Supporting Mathematical Development in the Early Years,* Milton Keynes: Open University Press.

- Brian Clegg, Slackcote Mill, Slackcote Lane, Delph, Oldham OL3 5TP Tel: 01457 785881. Suppliers of A-frames, ladders, storage trolleys, etc.

- Community Playthings for an excellent range of long-lasting equipment including playcubes and different sized blocks, www.communityplaythings.co.uk.

- DIY and home ware stores are a treasure trove for possibilities of play materials to wander round and get inspiration. Look in your local area. Some examples include: www.diy.com, www.homebase.co.uk, www.ikea.com, www.timberline.co.uk and www.therange.co.uk.

- Galt Educational Resource Catalogue: www.galteducational.co.uk

📖 Lewisham Early Years Advice and Resource Network (2002) A Place to Learn: Developing a Stimulating Environment. Copies of this publication can be obtained from LEARN Tel: 020 8695 9806 Email: eys.advisers@lewisham.gov.uk.

📖 Myriad Toys are a wonderful company selling play materials made from natural resources: www.myriad.online.co.uk.

📖 NES Arnold resource catalogue: www.nesarnold.co.uk.

🎵 Rhymes and songs from www.avidgroup.co.uk (Tumble Tots Action songs), www.kidsmusiceducation.com, www.songsforteaching.com/numberscounting.htm.

📖 Spectrum Educational, a small and excellent educational supplier www.spectrumeducational.net.

📖 Treeblocks (a selection of natural cuts and slices of tree trunks and branches) from www.treeblocks.com.

 The EYFS principles

The four principles which guide the work of all early years practitioners are discussed on pp. 31–33. Please refer to this for a greater understanding of how to put the principles into practice.

Shape, space and measures

From birth–11 months

What children have said or done

This observation, of a ten-month-old baby playing with an individual object from a treasure basket, demonstrates prolonged play and exploration of the textural qualities of the object.

> James was playing with his treasure basket. At ten months old, he was familiar with the objects, but on this day he picked out a gilt compact case. He held this flat, round and shiny metal object at arm's length away from himself and as he did so, the sunlight caught it and reflected in his face. He moved the object carefully, noticing the sparkly light coming and going. He began to make humming noises and then began to sway backwards and forwards.

Bringing the object to his mouth, James started to lick it gently with rasping sounds. In a little while he put the case on the carpeted floor and began gently pushing it backwards and forwards. This then turned into a hitting motion. The case slid almost out of reach, and James had to stretch out to touch it. He repeated this several times until it slid out of reach and James' attention turned to the other objects in the treasure basket.

The play with this single object lasted several minutes

Look, listen and note

- It is often felt that babies who are younger than twelve months old simply put things in their mouths when they play with objects. It is true that most babies, when picking up objects for the first time, do put them in their mouths. They are 'testing them out' through smell and taste, which are the most powerful senses for a young baby. As you observe babies more closely, you will see that they soon begin to look at objects much more closely, shake them, drop them and bang them against other objects.

- What babies are doing is noticing the shapes, sizes, weights, textures, colours, smells and temperature changes of different objects in the environment.

- Notice how carefully babies examine objects and how they may be cautious when picking up something for the first time. When objects become familiar they might grab them with gusto!

Activities, objects and rhymes

Discoveries throughout the day

Throughout the baby's day there is an ongoing opportunity for exploration and discovery:

- At nappy-changing time, offer babies objects to play with.

- When babies begin to eat with their fingers, the texture of different foods is a source of interest.

- When you carry babies about, walking in the nursery or in the garden, or even out and about, point things out to them, such as the leaves in the trees, the pictures on the walls, the curtains at the windows and so on. Allow the babies to reach out and touch these things, enjoying their different textures and shapes.

- During bathtime and water play there are wonderful opportunities for babies to experience the different qualities of water. Use containers with holes at the bottom such as different-sized flower pots, tea strainers and small sieves. Use small plastic jugs and teapots with spouts for pouring, so babies see different amounts of 'water flow'. Add foam bath or change the temperature of the water or add food colouring. Creating variations will add interest for the baby.

- Sensory play with wet and dry sand, gloop (cornflour and water), dried pasta, lentils, rice, etc., and containers for pouring, all offer opportunities for discovering the forms and textures of different material.

- The objects in a treasure basket offer a wealth of opportunity to experience shape, form and texture of objects (see Chapter 6).

Here is a quote from my book on early play describing the potential for learning with objects.

> Babies learn a range of concepts to do with the physical qualities of objects, such as coldness, smoothness, heaviness and prickliness. They also begin to recognise that some objects are rigid and others move about between their fingers. They notice that some objects are hollow and some objects are solid. They experience the transparency of glass and the reflective nature of shiny metal. They experience the fact that some objects change temperature as you hold them and some do not ... that some material has a strong scent, such as leather, rubber or lemon, whereas the scent of wicker, bristle or stone is less potent.
>
> (Hughes 2006: 34)

Nursery rhyme

Five Fat Peas

Five fat peas in a pea pod pressed
[Hold hand in fist.]
One grew, two grew, so did all the rest.
[Put thumb and fingers up one by one.]
They grew and grew
[Raise hand in the air very slowly.]
And did not stop,
Until one day
The pod went POP!
[Clap hands together.]

Effective practice

Be on the lookout to ensure a baby is being offered the opportunity to explore a variety of objects during different times of the day. Whilst we normally put plastic objects in water, consider, for example, introducing other material such as sponges, metal objects and wooden objects, so the baby experiences absorption, sinking and floating.

It is also important for babies to see what the adult is doing during the normal everyday routines, whether it is putting washing in a washing machine, preparing milk in a feeding bottle or setting the table. Babies are curious and observant. When they are on the move, they will want to copy the things we do. Babies make sense of the world through their senses and their eyes are drawn to the key adults in their lives. Talk to the babies and tell them what you are doing; give them the feeling that they are part of your life.

Planning and resourcing

- Make sure there is the opportunity for a quiet time each day to offer the treasure basket, when you can sit close by to be attentive and responsive to the babies.

- Singing nursery rhymes to babies is at the heart of social play and part of the way we pass our culture from one generation to the next. Take every opportunity to have fun with singing when you are on your own with babies at the intimate times such as nappy-changing or cuddle times.

Home links

- Many parents appreciate the value of nursery rhymes but lack confidence in singing them. Support parents in this by sharing their babies' favourite rhymes and lending them nursery-rhyme books.

- Babies are not able to share with their parents what they have enjoyed or maybe what has upset them during the day (like older children can). Practitioners need to create time to give feedback to parents at the end of the day. Similarly, it is good for parents to share with a baby's key person anything important that has happened since the baby's last session when they arrive in the morning.

Additional resources

- Goldschmied, E. (1986) *Infants at Work: Babies of 6–9 Months Exploring Everyday Objects* (Film), London: National Children's Bureau. (Reproduced on DVD in 2007.)

- Goldschmied, E. and Jackson, S. (2003) *People Under Three: Young Children in Day Care,* 2nd edn, London: Routledge.

📖 Hughes, A. M. (2006) *Developing Play for the Under Threes: The Treasure Basket and Heuristic Play,* London: David Fulton Publishers.

📖 Lindon, J. (2006) *Helping Babies and Toddlers Learn: A Guide to Good Practice with Under Threes,* 2nd edn, London: National Children's Bureau.

🎵 Rhymes and Songs from www.kidsmusiceducation.com

📖 Treasure baskets can be made to order from P. H. Coate and Son, www.englishwillowbaskets.co.uk. Treasure basket sets can be ordered from Early Excellence, www.earlyexcellence.com.

From 8–26 months

Development matters

- Find out what toys are like and can do through handling objects.

- Recognise big things and small things in meaningful contexts.

- Attempt, sometimes successfully, to fit shapes into spaces on inset boards or jigsaw puzzles.

- Use blocks to create their own simple structures and arrangements.

- Enjoy filling and emptying containers.

Key words

filling and emptying

What children have said or done

The following observation illustrates how a fifteen-month-old boy is discovering how shapes fit (or don't fit) into spaces, through trial and error, a little help from his key person Kelly and plenty of open-ended play material.

Tom has chosen to play with the plastic bottles, pebbles, corks and shells. I am sitting near to him on a comfortable low chair. He knows that I am there because at first he keeps looking at me and smiling. Now he is engrossed in his play. He picks up a pebble and tries to fit it in the neck of a bottle but the pebble is too large. He picks up another pebble but this is the wrong shape as well. He then finds a tin and begins to fill the tin with the pebbles. Tom picks up the plastic bottle and finds a cork. He successfully pushes the cork in the wide neck of the bottle and begins to shake the bottle. He successfully repeats this with another cork. The third cork, which he chooses, is a champagne cork but this is too fat to fit in the neck. Tom keeps trying to fit it in without success. I pick up a smaller cork and hand it to him. Initially he shakes his head and ignores my outstretched hand. I am careful not to speak. I do not want to interrupt his play and concentration. In a few seconds, he drops the champagne cork and takes the one I have offered to him. He successfully pushes it through the neck and turns round giving me a big grin. I do speak this time! Tom shakes his bottle. It makes a good sound because it has three corks in it now.

 ## *Look, listen and note*

In the observation described in the previous section, Tom is discovering for himself how shapes fit into spaces. When you are providing containers and objects to children, notice their discoveries about how things fit into one another.

At this age, inset boards and jigsaw puzzles have limited interest as there is only chance for one success in the 'space'. Open-ended material and containers or tubes offer the chance for more extended play and exploration and the development of the placing tool.

Children like to repeat activity over and over again when they discover that something 'happens'. Notice how the children repeat an action in their play. This is how they learn.

Activities, objects and rhymes

Heuristic play

Children of this age are naturally curious about what they can do with objects. They are developing the learning tools of placing, piling, banging and pairing (see Chapter 4, pp. 27–28).

In their play, children want to fill and empty containers and pile objects one on top of the other. This kind of play is called heuristic play and has been described in Chapter 4 (pp. 28–30). I have described how you can set up for a heuristic-play session and provided a suggested list of objects and containers in Chapter 6 (pp. 45–48)

Opportunities for heuristic play allow young children to experiment with and to understand how different shapes and sizes will fit into spaces.

Playing with blocks

Blocks are probably one of the most important pieces of play equipment you can have in your setting. They have play value for babies from six months old to children of school age and upwards. When children are

Two boys playing with blocks I

playing with blocks, they are developing the placing and piling learning tools.

Blocks can be obtained in all sizes from a variety of different sources such as educational suppliers and toy shops. They can be manufactured in wood or plastic, although wood is the preferred material.

You can also make your own blocks from sanded offcuts of wood from a builder's merchant or wood donated by parents or local builders. However, such blocks need to be sanded to a satin-smooth finish to avoid splinters.

How children might play with blocks

- banging two blocks together;
- piling blocks one on top of another to make a tower and then knocking them down;
- filling containers such as tins and boxes with blocks;
- lining blocks along the floor;
- creating two parallel rows of blocks to make a 'road';
- creating a simple building structure;

Two boys playing with blocks II

- creating 'contained' areas with a single layer of blocks to make a 'house', 'zoo', 'beach', etc.;

- making patterns fit together with different shaped blocks;

- creating 'worlds' with blocks, such as a 'dinosaur world' using small dinosaur figures;

- building dens using large blocks;

- creating obstacle courses.

 ## Nursery rhyme

Five Little Seashells

Five little seashells
[Hold out five fingers.]
Lying on the shore.
[Open your other hand and pass it over the five fingers.]
Swish went the waves.
[Make a tight fist with the first hand and pass the open hand back over the first.]
And then there were four.

Two boys playing with blocks III

Two boys playing with blocks IV

[Hold out four fingers. Continue these actions for the following verses.]

Four little seashells, pretty as can be.
Swish went the waves. Then there were three.
Three little seashells, all pearly new.
Swish went the waves. Then there were two.
Two little seashells, lying in the sun.
Swish went the waves. Then there was one.
One little seashell, lying all alone.
I picked it up.
[Point one finger in the air.]
I took it home.
[Put it in your pocket.]

By Hugh Hanley,
www.songsforteaching.com/hughhanley/5littleseashells.htm

Effective practice

- Blocks need to be available for children to play with every day and are ideal play material both indoors and outdoors.

- As toddlers begin to develop language, introduce vehicles, toy animals or figures with the block play as this will extend the opportunities for them to develop their play.

Planning and resourcing

- It is a good idea to have a large number of blocks (preferably wooden) which can be stored and made available in a special dedicated area in the playroom or outside play area.

- When using wood offcuts, make sure that they are sanded well so there is no chance of children getting splinters or scratched.

- Heuristic-play materials are best stored as separate collections of objects in fairly large drawstring bags. These can then be either hung up for easy access or stored in a cupboard.

Home links

- Talk with your parents about the value of heuristic play and block play. You could take photos, invite parents to come into your setting and observe their children at play.

- Invite parents to add to your collection of heuristic-play materials or provide sanded wood offcuts if they have anything suitable. It not only will help enhance your setting but also will give the parents more confidence about the safety and suitability of this kind of everyday material. When parents are more involved, they feel more of a part of their children's learning in your setting.

Additional resources

- Goldschmied, E. and Hughes, A. M. (1992) *Heuristic Play with Objects* (Film), London: National Children's Bureau (reproduced on DVD in 2007).

- Hughes, A. M. (2006) *Developing Play for the Under Threes: The Treasure Basket and Heuristic Play,* London: David Fulton Publishers.

- Lindon, J. (2006) *Helping Babies and Toddlers to Learn: A Guide to Good Practice with Under Threes,* 2nd edn, London: National Children's Bureau.

- Heuristic play materials can be ordered from Early Excellence, www.earlyexcellence.com.

- Community Playthings for an excellent range of long-lasting wooden blocks of all sizes, www.communityplaythings.co.uk.

- Rhymes and songs from www.kidsmusiceducation.com

From 22–36 months

Development matters

- Notice simple shapes and patterns in pictures.
- Begin to categorise objects according to properties such as shape and size.
- Are beginning to understand variations in size.

Key words

noticing shapes and size

What children have said or done

Daniel is nearly two and a half years old, and this is what his key person Jenny wrote about her general observations of his interests in numbers and measures:

> Daniel is now beginning to understand and talk about different sizes. He can fetch the big car or the small toy dinosaurs if I ask him but he does not use the terms 'big' or 'small' himself. He usually refers to things as Daniel- or Jenny-sized.
>
> Daniel likes to organise things in lines. He will line up blocks, cars, coins, toys, animals and so on. He also likes to find a group of identical or similar objects in a pot or container, then empty them out and refill the container. He is not actively separating or sorting different things out for himself yet.

Look, listen and note

- Children develop in very different ways at this stage. Some children can demonstrate very advanced language development and want to talk to you about the shapes and sizes of objects because they find it interesting. Other children prefer to actively 'play around' with objects and although they may not yet have the language of 'round', 'square', 'big' or 'little', for example, these features will be meaningful to them from the direct experience they have had through their play.

- Shapes and sizes are two features that we need to be aware of to develop numeracy and problem-solving skills. They are important in everyday tasks such as knowing how to efficiently stack different-sized boxes of toys in a cupboard.

- Sorting develops from having experience of playing with groups of identical or similar objects.

Activities, objects and rhymes

The potential of the cardboard box

Let us consider the humble cardboard box. It is an object that is part of all our lives. Most items we purchase are contained in cardboard boxes. The age-old story which everyone likes to tell is how children will open up a box to find their new toys, only to discard the toys in favour of the box. Cardboard boxes can become a key part of the play resources you provide for the children both indoors and outdoors.

Features of cardboard boxes

- they are readily available;

- they can be obtained free of charge;

- they are easily replaced (this is necessary because they disintegrate quickly);

- they come in all shapes and sizes;

- they are safe;

- they can be cut and painted;

- they can have other objects stuck or secured to them.

How cardboard boxes can be used

- as containers for filling and emptying;

- as containers for sorting;

- as posting boxes;

- as containers for 'feely' items;

- for the role play as items in the kitchen or for shopping;

- to create imaginary 'containers', such as a cot, train, boat or castle;

- for modelling using glue and paint, etc.;

- for creating imaginary 'scenes' with animals, figures, dolls-house furniture, etc.;

- for making dens and tunnels.

The fantastic value of a cardboard box cannot be measured because playing with them allows children to extend their learning and skills in all areas of the EYFS and not just in the area of 'problem-solving, reasoning and numeracy' skills. Boxes are an ideal resource for children to engage with their main schemas (patterns of behaviour) of containing, connecting, transporting and enveloping. (See Chapter 1, pp. 8–10 for more information about schemas.)

Some suggestions of cardboard boxes

- large boxes for electrical items such as a washing machine or furniture;

- shoe boxes of various sizes (plus their lids);

- chocolate boxes;

- toy packaging boxes;

- match boxes;

- cereal boxes and other food packaging boxes;

- jewellery boxes;

- stationery boxes;

- tissue boxes;

- wine boxes;

- toiletries boxes;

- pizza-delivery boxes.

The possibilities are endless!

The role-play area

Very young children are particularly interested in pretending to do what the grown-ups do and also to behave like them. They enjoy pretending to do domestic activities which are familiar, and every playroom should have a role-play area for this age upwards.

The role-play area provides many opportunities for young children to learn about numbers, shapes and measures. These might include sorting plates by colour or size, setting the table or pegging out clothes on a washing line or stand.

Some suggested resources for the role-play area

- packaging in a variety of shapes and sizes;

- pairs of shoes;

- different-sized clothes items, such as socks and vests;

- plates and bowls of different sizes.

See section 40–60 months (pp. 134–135) for further resources.

Storage

The way you store play material can offer opportunities for matching and sorting according to shape and size. Using silhouettes of the different shapes and sizes of play material on your shelves or some floor areas is an excellent way for children to 'notice' these features for themselves.

Giant naming and categorising game

For a group of two to three children.

Skills

- Practising taking turns.

- Learning about the relationships between common objects.

- Learning about concepts and categories.

- Learning about shapes and sizes.

Materials you will need

- Three A2 sheets of cardboard.

- A selection of pictures from the categories of animals, clothing and food.

Preparation

- Cover each of the boards with the pictures from one of the three categories to about 60 per cent of its area, leaving a suitable space for placing picture cards.

- Laminate the completed boards.

- Collect a set of twenty-four large picture cards (approximately postcard size) of single items, eight from each category.

Activity

You can play this game with an individual child or with a small group.

- In a group, the children take turns at picking up a card from the set, naming the object, its category and describing its shape and size then placing the card in the space on the appropriate board.

- The game continues until either all cards have been picked up or when the children lose interest.

You can extend this game by encouraging the children to talk about the pictures. For example, a picture of a shoe may lead to a discussion of the footwear of the group. The same method can be used with an individual child.

Nursery rhyme

Shapes All Around Us

Shapes, shapes,
Shapes all around us.
Shapes, shapes,
Shapes all around us.
So many different shapes to share
So many different shapes to share.
First there is the circle
Round as can be.
Then there is the square,
Four equal sides has he.
A triangle has three sides,
No matter what the lengths.
A rectangle has two long sides
But short on each end.

By David Burba and Lisa Campbell,
www.songsforteaching.com/math/geometry/shapes.htm

Effective practice

- When providing objects and resources for the role-play area, it is best if you can use 'real' items (rather than toy versions).

- You may find that your role-play area is too small and is getting too crowded. Observe how the children use this area and expand it, if necessary. Maybe have two role-play areas in one playroom.

- Observing children in the role-play area gives you a lot of insight into children's mathematical learning as well as their emotional well-being and level of social skills. However, you need to be discreet and unobtrusive for children to play freely and unself-consciously.

Planning and resourcing

- When using cardboard boxes, you may like to clear a space in which to put several boxes and simply let the children choose how they want to play with them.

- Cardboard boxes are quickly torn or flattened, and storage of boxes takes up a lot of space. Unless it is a fantastic large box that you want to keep for a while, don't be afraid to discard them in your recycling bank. You can always collect more.

Home links

- Ask parents to bring in boxes.

- Take photos of the children playing with boxes to show their parents how much pleasure and learning they have gained.

- Share the observations you have made of the children in the role-play area.

- Encourage parents to talk to their children about the different shapes and sizes of objects at home.

Additional resources

- Community Playthings for a range of long-lasting large and small wooden blocks, www.communityplaythings.co.uk.

- Myriad toys for a wonderful selection of play material made out of natural resources, www.myriad.online.co.uk.

- Rhymes and songs from www.songsforteaching.com/numberscounting.htm.

From 30–50 months

Development matters

- Show an interest in shape and space by playing with shapes or making arrangements with objects.

- Show awareness of similarities in shapes in the environment.

- Observe and use positional language.

- Are beginning to understand 'bigger than' and 'enough'.

- Show interest in shape by sustained construction activity or by talking about shapes or arrangements.

- Use shapes appropriately for tasks.

- Begin to talk about the shapes of everyday objects.

Key words

interest in shapes, arrangements and construction

What children have said or done

The focus of this chapter is about children's awareness of shapes and sizes, which develops through active involvement in domestic tasks, such as cooking and shopping with parents and key persons. The way we use language is important in supporting children in their learning. Learning about categorising happens through 'sorting' play. However, children often have 'their own ideas' about how to categorise objects as can be seen from this parental report of Helen, who is just four years old.

> Helen seems to classify things according to their function, rather than shapes, colours or sizes. For example, her toys (which include common objects borrowed from around the house) will be arranged into 'kitchen set' (pots, stirring things, etc.), 'baby set' (small blanket, doll, cushions, cardboard boxes for baby's food, etc.), 'doctor set' (various nondescript jars and spoons used as check up tools), 'the

market' (bags, purse with money, notebook, a variety of random things we don't use any more to 'buy and sell'). Helen also likes to sort out the fruit and vegetables after we have been shopping.

Look, listen and note

- It is fun to observe children in their play and see their different interests. They will have 'their own ideas', and it is good to notice these and encourage them as it supports independent thinking and curiosity.

- Notice how children begin to describe 'where things are' and 'what they look like' and be responsive and show an interest in what they are telling and showing you.

Activities, objects and rhymes

Playing outside

It is really important for children to have the opportunity to play outside all the year round. Even a narrow concrete yard can be turned into a 'heuristic play' type of environment but on a larger scale. You just have to use your imagination to provide a range of open-ended everyday materials that allow children plenty of opportunities for problem-solving and experimenting with shapes and space.

In the next section 40–60 months (pp. 137–139) I have set out some suggestions, which are relevant for this age group as well.

Further ideas for playing outside can be found in Chapter 7 in the 40–60 months section (pp. 96–98).

Sorting

Sorting activity increases children's awareness of similarities in shapes and other visual features in the environment.

Sorting activity needs to be something that children can choose to do themselves, although you will need to make the objects and containers for sorting clearly available.

By increasing the number of objects from two to many, they functionally become 'sets'. Sorting is about making collections of things into sets.

Some more ideas of objects for sorting

- buttons
- corks
- bottle tops
- pom-poms
- tins
- pebbles
- beads
- feathers
- hair rollers

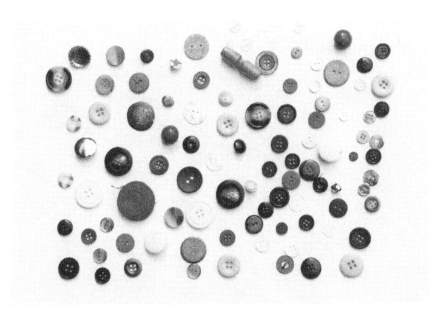

Buttons

- assorted balls
- cardboard tubes
- coloured pasta
- coloured pencils
- fir cones
- baskets
- drinking straws
- pea shingle.

I Spy walks

When you take children out for a walk, encourage them to look out for different shapes, patterns and qualities in the things they see. Look out for:

- diagonal lines
- straight lines
- curved lines

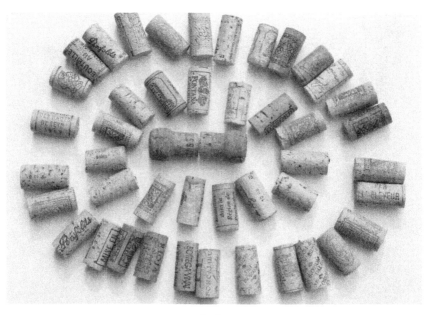

Corks

- circles

- squares

- triangles

- rectangles

- glass, wood, metal things

- things that move, new, broken, rusty things

- wet, shiny, rough, delicate, old.

Shape Lotto game

For a group of two to four children.

Skills

- Learning about shape names.

- Practising matching shapes.

- Turn taking in a small group.

Stones

Materials you will need

- Four flat boards, each covered with printed shapes of different colours and sizes, so that one board has circles, one board has squares, one board has rectangles and one board has triangles.

- Each board has a suitable marked space for the picture cards.

- A set of forty clear picture cards of single shapes, ten of each shape in different sizes and colours.

Activity

- The boards are placed in front of the children.

- Name the shapes together and then place the cards face down in the middle.

- The children then take turns at picking a card from the pack, naming the shape, colour and size on the image and placing it in the space on the appropriate board.

- You can continue the game until the cards have all been used or until the children look as if they have had enough.

- The same method can be used for one child.

 Nursery rhyme

Circles go 'round and 'round

Circles go 'round and 'round,
Circles go 'round and 'round,
No corners, no sides,
Circles go round and round.
Squares have four corners,
Squares have four sides,
All corners are the same,
All sides are the same.
Rectangles have four corners and four sides,
Two sides are short,
Two sides are long.

Triangles have three corners and three sides,
Sides and corners
Can be of any size.
Circles go 'round and 'round,
No corners, no sides,
Circles go 'round and 'round.

By Jennifer Fixman, www.songsforteaching.com/
jennyfixmanedutunes/circlesgoroundand round.htm.

Effective practice

- When playing structured games or activities try to 'sense' when the children have lost interest. At first you may not realise it as children tend to cooperate and want to please adults. However, if you need to encourage them a lot and they resist your ideas, walk away or seem a bit lifeless then these are signs that they have had enough.

- Keep your objects for sorting in clearly labelled containers and make sure that they can be accessed easily.

Planning and resourcing

- It is tempting to buy manufactured 'sorting toys', but collections of objects that you have made will be much more satisfying both to you and to the children.

- When making lotto games, it is a good idea to laminate the boards and cards or cover them in sticky-back plastic. You will then need to find appropriate containers for them, which are clearly labelled.

Home links

- Share with parents any new language the children have learnt or are using and encourage them to play lotto type games with them at home.

- Show the parents your 'sorting' collections of objects and encourage them to make 'sorting' collections for their children at home. Maybe parents could help you with your collections?

Additional resources

Rhymes and songs from

♫ www.avidgroup.co.uk (Tumble Tots Action Songs)

♫ www.songsforteaching.com/numberscounting.htm

♫ www.KidsMusicEducation.com

See list of additional resources at the end of the '40–60 months' section (pp. 141–142) for many ideas.

From 40–60 months

Development matters

- Show curiosity about and observation of shapes by talking about how they are same and different.

- Match some shapes by recognising similarities and orientation.

- Begin to use mathematical names for 'solid' three-dimensional shapes and 'flat' two-dimensional shapes and mathematical terms to describe shapes.

- Select a particular named shape.

- Show awareness of symmetry.

- Find items from positional or directional clues.

- Order two or three items by length or weight.

- Order two items by weight or capacity.

- Match sets of objects to numerals that represent the number of objects.

- Sort familiar objects to identify their similarities and differences, making choices and justifying decisions.

- Describe solutions to practical problems, drawing on experience, talking about own ideas, methods and choices.

- Use familiar objects and common shapes to create and recreate patterns and build models.

- Use everyday language related to time, order and sequence familiar events and measure short periods of time with a non-standard unit, for example with a sand timer.

- Count how many objects share a particular property, presenting results using pictures, drawings or numerals.

Early learning goals

- Use language such as 'greater', 'smaller', 'heavier' or 'lighter' to compare quantities.

- Talk about, recognise and recreate simple patterns.

- Use language such as 'circle' or 'bigger' to describe the shape and size of solids and flat shapes.

- Use everyday words to describe position.

- Use developing mathematical ideas and methods to solve practical problems.

Key words

shape names, measurement and sorting

What children have said or done

Ben is four years old and enjoys cooking with his mother. This is what she wrote about his understanding of number and measurement.

> Ben enjoys helping with cooking especially when I am baking things like cakes, which involves talking about numbers as well as doing a succession of tasks. Under direction he will fill three cups with flour, one cup with milk and one with sugar. He will count and break eggs and will add ingredients spoonful by spoonful.
>
> Ben knows what scales are for but he can't yet understand the exact meaning of weights. However he does know that the hand tells you how heavy something is. He has the experience of weights and measures when he carries a litre of milk or a kilo of flour and we talk about things being heavier or lighter. He also knows ingredients and food by category and likes to put the cinnamon with the spices, the basil with the herbs, the pot of baking powder next to the flour and so on.

Look, listen and note

- Children love to help adults in domestic tasks, and in the above observation you can see how the simple act of baking offers many opportunities to learn about numbers and measurement.

- Make sure that you talk to the children as they play or help you in tasks as this will extend their language, knowledge and understanding of numbers and shapes.

- Point out to children the shapes of objects in their surroundings, name their positions and generally enjoy the children's increasing awareness and interest in numerical and positional features.

- Notice the children's language and enjoy discussing their ideas with them and extending their language development.

Activities, objects and rhymes

There are many opportunities that you can create to give the children of pre-school age experiences that enhance their understanding of shapes, time, positions in space and counting. These opportunities can be provided through:

* adult-directed activity such as board, card or treasure-hunt games with rules;

* domestic tasks such as cooking and setting up or tidying up the play material;

* providing a stimulating environment both indoors and outdoors so the children can make their own discoveries in their freely chosen play;

* singing, dancing, talking and storytelling.

Here are some ideas for you to try. You may have tried some before, some are new and some are part of your everyday routine. Whatever they are, make sure that the children are fully engaged and that you share in their pleasure, pride and enjoyment.

Food preparation

Why not try this simple idea in your setting. It involves no cooking, but there is plenty of cutting and talking about numbers and shapes!

Harry Hedgehog melon

Materials you will need

* a melon (cut in half, so it will lie flat on a plate)

* a small tin of pineapple chunks

* about 250 grams of cheddar cheese

* two stuffed olives

* cocktail sticks.

Activity

- Make Harry's eyes out of the stuffed olives and stick on to cocktail sticks. Insert at one end of the melon.

- Under supervision, the children can cut the cheese into cubes using short bladed knives which are sharp enough to cut through easily.

- Put the pineapple chunks and cheese cubes together on cocktail sticks and stick them all over the melon so they look like the spines of a hedgehog.

This activity is fun and offers opportunities to talk about numbers, sizes and shapes.

The role-play area

I have already referred to the role-play area on p. 118. As children become more sophisticated in their language and social skills, you can introduce further resources to reflect that development. The following items will promote all areas of mathematical development.

Further suggested resources for the role-play area

- alarm clock and wall clock;

- diaries, calendars and notebooks;

- telephone and telephone directories;

- parcels of different shapes, sizes and weights for a 'post office' theme;

- a weighing machine or balancing scales;

- cooked salt dough food to weigh, count or size;

- recipe cards or books;

- vegetable rack and fruit basket to sort fruit and vegetables;

- dolls of various sizes and their clothes (can be matched by size);

- dressing-up clothes, hats, bags and baskets (can be matched by size and shape);

- hairdressing materials including empty shampoo and conditioner bottles;

- various sizes of cutlery, plates, bowls, bread baskets, etc.;

- place mats and tablecloths of different shapes and sizes.

Measuring activities

- **Draw round bodies**. Using lengths from a roll of plain wallpaper, draw round the children as they lie down on the paper with a thick black felt pen. Cut out the silhouette shapes and mount them around the room on the wall so the children can compare their heights and shapes.

- **Roll down the slope**. If you have a slope in your garden or nearby park you might like to try out this activity. Each child rolls down the slope and you can mark the point each child reaches. Then you can measure how far each child has rolled using the children's feet, walking heel to toe and counting. You may also want to use measuring sticks.

- **Weather charts**. You can create your own daily weather chart, which could include noticing and recording whether it is sunny, cloudy, raining, snowing or frosty. You could also measure the temperature and have a bucket to collect rainwater, the depth of which could be measured if you have a heavy rainstorm.

- **Cable spool game**. This is a good measuring game for playing outside. Lay out a long sheet of plain wallpaper. The children then take turns rolling the cable spool along the paper and measuring the distance travelled. You may want to use a small ramp at the start to get the spool going.

Shape activities

Fruit and vegetable patterns

Day 1
Bring into your setting the following:

- a red cabbage

- an onion

- an orange

- an apple

- a green pepper

- a walnut.

Have the children in a small group look at the outside of each piece of fruit or vegetable. Encourage them to describe the shape, texture and markings. Ask them questions such as:

- Which one is purple? Red? Brown?

- Which ones are smooth? Bumpy?

- Which one pulls apart?

- Which one is crackly and feels like paper?

- Which one has tiny spots on its skin?

Offer a magnifying glass for closer examination. Leave the fruits and vegetables out for free inspection during the day.

Day 2
The next day, you can ask the children to predict what each piece will look like when it is cut open.

- Which will be the same colour inside?

- Will there be seeds?

Now cut them open and talk together about what you discover. It is best to cut them around the 'waist' of the fruits not at their 'tops and bottoms'.

Leaf patterns

- Bring in a couple of small branches with leaves on them.

- Ask a small group of children to describe whatever they notice. Then encourage them to examine the branch more closely, noticing patterns or marks in the bark or leaves, their colour, size, spaces between the leaves, etc.

- Ask questions such as:

  - How are the leaves attached to the branch?

  - Are they like your arms, straight across or do they zigzag?

  - Are all the lines straight? Are any of them diagonals?

- Cut the leaves off the branches so the children can sort them.

Playing outside

It is possible to play outside all year round if you resource your outdoor play area well. The opportunities for problem-solving, playing around with numbers, shapes and measuring can be done on a grander scale when you are outside, and the children love this kind of challenge.

Many play activities involve building things, which are the piling and brick-building learning tools in action. They also involve planning skills as well as a willingness to experiment and explore. Some building ideas might include:

- building a bridge using crates and planks (see photograph on p. 138); ©

- building a den using boxes, blocks, A frames, wooden clothes horse, sheets;

- building a 'house' or 'garage' for toy figures or cars, using boxes, bricks, wood offcuts, etc.;

- building a construction using crates, boxes, blocks, bricks and guttering to create steep or shallow slopes for small wheeled toys, balls, water, dry sand, etc. to slide down.

This kind of activity is often played by two or more children together, which leads to wonderful opportunities for developing language skills, cooperation and negotiating skills.

Children playing on crates and planks

Use of phrases such as 'bigger than', 'smaller than', 'longer than', 'thinner than', 'wider than' come naturally during this kind of play, and older children will model this language for younger children.

Further language such as 'under', 'on top of', 'behind', 'near', 'further away', 'in between', 'in the middle', 'next to', etc., is also practised during this kind of play.

Some further ideas for tools and props to play with outside

- gardening tools:
  - spades
  - forks
  - shovels
  - watering cans (the real versions are much more fun and work much better than toy versions);
- decorator's tools:
  - pots
  - large brushes
  - paint rollers;

- builder's tools:
  - spirit levels
  - pulleys
  - spanners
  - tape measures
  - measuring sticks;
- laminated numbers, pegs and washing line;
- woodwork bench with offcuts of wood, hammers, nails, pieces of sand paper (only suitable for children over three years old and under supervision at all times);
- large-scale games or giant dice;
- magnetic numbers and board;
- number beanbags;
- weather station.

 ## Nursery rhyme

The Shape Train

Come on everybody,
Let's get on board,
Shape, shape, shape train.
Come on everybody,
Let's get on board,
Shape, shape, shape train.
Round and round
Like a spinning wheel.
Circle, circle,
Get on board.
Four sides, four sides,
All the same.
Square, square,
Get on board.
Three sides, three sides,
Like a piece of pizza.

Triangle, triangle,
Get on board.
Four sides, four sides,
Like a cereal box.
Rectangle, rectangle,
Get on board.
Shape, shape, shape, train
Shape, shape, shape train.

By Ron Brown,
www.songsforteaching.com/intellitunes/shapetrain.htm

Effective practice

- When you are doing an activity like cooking or examining leaves or doing a measuring activity, keep the number of children you work with to no more than four at a time.

- When children are using scissors, knives or woodwork tools they need to be taught how to use them and then supervised closely. However it is essential that children have experience in using sharp bladed tools, so they become skilled and safe users before they reach school age.

Planning and resourcing

- Cooking and preparing food with children is fun, but you need to make sure that you have enough knives, spoons, bowls and chopping boards, etc., for each child to have his or her own to work with. Children also prefer adult-sized and 'real' materials.

- Many activities can take place both indoors and outdoors, so it is important to take the opportunity to go outdoors whenever possible.

- Children of this age love to be given new ideas and learning experiences through the 'activities' you can offer. However, make

sure there is always plenty of open-ended, everyday material available both indoors and outdoors for the children to freely explore
and experiment with throughout the day.

Home links

- Some parents may need reassurance that their children are safe when using sharp tools or kitchen utensils or playing with large outdoor equipment.

- Writing 'learning stories' and taking photos are lovely ways to share experiences with parents (see Carr 2001).

- Sometimes the children may want to take home the things they have made, drawn or cooked. Encourage parents to talk with their children about the things they bring home.

Additional resources

Baratta-Lorton, M. (ed.) (1998) *Mathematics Their Way: An Activity-Centred Mathematics Programme for Early Childhood,* Boston, Mass.: Addison Wesley Longman.

Bayley, R. and Broadbent, L. (2001) *50 Exciting Things to Do Outside,* Lawrence Educational Publications.

Bilton, H. (2004) *Playing Outside: Activities, Ideas and Inspiration for the Early Years,* London: David Fulton Publishers.

Carr, M. (2001) *Assessment in Early Childhood Settings,* London: Sage.

Featherstone, S. (2001) *The Little Book of Outdoor Play,* Leicester: Featherstone Education Ltd.

Lewisham Early Years Advice and Resource Network (2002) *A Place to Learn: Developing a Stimulating Environment,* London: Lewisham Early Years Advice and Resource Network.

📖 Pound, L. (1999) *Supporting Mathematical Development in the Early Years,* Milton Keynes: Open University Press.

📖 Asco Educational Supplies Ltd, www.ascoeducational.co.uk.

📖 Community Playthings for an excellent range of long lasting equipment including play cubes and different-sized blocks, www.communityplaythings.co.uk.

📖 DIY and homeware stores are a treasure trove for possibilities as play materials to wander round and get inspiration. Look in your local area. Some examples include www.diy.com, www.homebase.co.uk, www.ikea.com, www.timberline.co.uk, www.therange.co.uk.

📖 Galt Educational Resource Catalogue, www.galteducational.co.uk.

📖 Myriad Toys are a wonderful company selling play materials made from natural resources: www.myriad.online.co.uk.

📖 NES Arnold resource catalogue: www.nesarnold.co.uk.

🎵 Rhymes and songs from www.avidgroup.co.uk (Tumble Tots Action songs), www.KidsMusicEducation.com, www.songsforteaching.com/numberscounting.htm.

📖 Spectrum Educational, a small and excellent educational supplier, www.spectrumeducational.net.

📖 Treeblocks (a selection of natural cuts and slices of tree trunks and branches) from www.treeblocks.com.

 # The EYFS principles

The four principles which guide the work of all early years practitioners are discussed on pp. 31–33. Please refer to this for a greater understanding of how to put the principles into practice.

References and further reading

Baratta-Lorton, M. (ed.) (1998) *Mathematics Their Way: An Activity-Centred Mathematics Programme for Early Childhood,* Boston: Addison Wesley Longman.

Bruce, T. (2001) *Learning Through Play: Babies, Toddlers and the Foundation Years,* London: Hodder and Stoughton.

Carr, M. (2001) *Assessment in Early Childhood Settings,* London: Sage.

Daly, M., Byers, E. and Taylor, W. (2006) *Understanding Early Years Theory in Practice,* Oxford: Heinemann.

Department for Education and Skills (DfES) (2003) *Effective Pre-School and Primary Education 3–11 Project,* Nottingham: DfES Publications.

——(2007a) *Statutory Framework for the Early Years Foundation Stage,* Nottingham: DfES Publications.

——(2007b) *Practice Guidance for the Early Years Foundation Stage,* Nottingham: DfES Publications.

Donaldson, M. (1978) *Children's Minds,* Glasgow: Fontana Collins.

Gellman, R. and Gallistel, C. R. (1978) *The Child's Understanding of Number,* Cambridge, Mass.: Harvard University Press.

Gerhardt, S. (2004) *Why Love Matters: How Affection Shapes a Baby's Brain,* Hove: Brunner-Routledge.

Goldschmied, E., Elfer, P. and Selleck, D. (2003) *Key Persons in the Nursery,* London: David Fulton

Goldschmied, E. and Jackson, S. (2003) *People Under Three: Young Children in Day Care,* 2nd edn, London: Routledge.

Hughes, A. M. (2006) *Developing Play for the Under Threes: The Treasure Basket and Heuristic Play,* London: David Fulton.

Lindon, J. (2001) *Understanding Children's Play,* Cheltenham: Nelson Thornes.

——(2005) *Understanding Child Development: Linking Theory and Practice,* London: Hodder Arnold.

Meadows, S. (1993) *The Child as Thinker,* London: Routledge.

Montessori, M. (1988) *The Absorbent Mind,* Oxford: Clio Press.

Munn, P. (1998) 'Symbolic Function in Pre-schoolers', in C. Donlan (ed.), *The Development of Mathematical Skills,* Hove: Psychology Press, pp. 47–71.

Piaget, J. (1973) 'Comments on Mathematical Education', in A. G. Howson (ed.), *Developments in Mathematical Education: Proceedings of the Second International Congress on Mathematical Education,* Cambridge: Cambridge University Press, pp. 79–87.

Robson, S. (2006) *Developing Thinking and Understanding in Young Children,* London: Routledge.

Siegler, R. S. and Alibali, M. W. (2005) *Children's Thinking,* 4th edn, Upper Saddle River, NJ: Pearson Prentice Hall.

Siegler, R. S., Deloache, J. and Eisenberg, N. (2003) *How Children Develop,* New York: Worth Publishers.

Siraj-Blatchford, I., Sylva, K., Muttock, S., Gilden, R. and Bell, D. (2002) *Researching Effective Pedagogy in the Early Years (Research Report 356),* London: DfES.

Sophian, C. (1998) 'The Developmental Perspective on Children's Counting', in C. Donlan (ed.), *The Development of Mathematical Skills,* Hove: Psychology Press, pp. 27–46.

Stroh, S., Robinson, T. and Proctor, A. (2008) *Every Child Can Learn: Using Learning Tools and Play to Help Children With Developmental Delay,* London: Sage.

Thornton, L. and Brunton, P. (2005) *Understanding the Reggio Approach,* London: David Fulton.

Vygotsky, L. (1978) *The Mind in Society,* Cambridge, Mass.: Harvard University Press.

White, J. (2002) *The Child's Mind,* London: RoutledgeFalmer.

Wynn, K. (1998) 'Numerical Competence in Infants', in C. Donlan (ed.), *The Development of Mathematical Skills,* Hove: Psychology Press, pp. 1–25.

eBooks – at www.eBookstore.tandf.co.uk

A library at your fingertips!

eBooks are electronic versions of printed books. You can store them on your PC/laptop or browse them online.

They have advantages for anyone needing rapid access to a wide variety of published, copyright information.

eBooks can help your research by enabling you to bookmark chapters, annotate text and use instant searches to find specific words or phrases. Several eBook files would fit on even a small laptop or PDA.

NEW: Save money by eSubscribing: cheap, online access to any eBook for as long as you need it.

Annual subscription packages

We now offer special low-cost bulk subscriptions to packages of eBooks in certain subject areas. These are available to libraries or to individuals.

For more information please contact webmaster.ebooks@tandf.co.uk

We're continually developing the eBook concept, so keep up to date by visiting the website.

www.eBookstore.tandf.co.uk

Lightning Source UK Ltd.
Milton Keynes UK
UKOW06f1810300815

257793UK00003B/217/P